5/02

# humor me

WITHDRAWN

# humor me

●

## AN ANTHOLOGY
## OF HUMOR BY WRITERS
## OF COLOR

### Edited by John McNally

University of Iowa Press
Iowa City

University of Iowa Press, Iowa City 52242

http://www.uiowa.edu/~uipress

The publication of this book was generously supported by
the University of Iowa Foundation.

Printed on acid-free paper

Library of Congress
Cataloging-in-Publication Data
Humor me: an anthology of humor by writers of color /
edited by John McNally.
p.      cm.
ISBN 0-87745-808-1 (pbk.)
1. American literature—Minority authors.    2. Ethnic
groups—Literary collections.    3. Minorities—Literary
collections.    4. Humorous stories, American.
5. Humorous poetry, American.    6. Ethnic groups—
Humor.    7. Minorities—Humor.    I. McNally, John,
1965–    .
PS508.M54 H86 2002
817.008′0920693—dc21          2001054842

02   03   04   05   06   P   5   4   3   2   1

Drawings on part-title pages by Paco Felici

IN MEMORY
of Beth and Chloe, the straight man and the comedian
of the pack, and our constant companions.
You are greatly missed.

# contents

## part three: cartoons and a graphic story

## part four: nonfiction

## part five: drama

# acknowledgments

First and foremost, I must thank my students at the University of Wisconsin-Madison who enrolled in "Voices of Humor in American Literature." There is no way I could have survived the short notice of teaching that course if not for those students, a group of promising scholars and budding humorists who braved the bait-and-switch of my appearance with their own piercing insights, articulate opinions, and boundless enthusiasm. My thanks to each and every one of them.

Thanks are also in order to the following for offering suggestions, helping with permissions, and/or being decent citizens in the world of literature: Sarah Walz, Ted Genoways, Darrel Simmons, Christine Aguila, Richard Peabody, Thea Kuticka of Bilingual Press, Jim Harris and Paul Ingram of Prairie Lights Bookstore in Iowa City, Christy Cox of FallsApart Productions, and Carol Bender at Alma College.

This is the fourth book for which my friend Scott Mackay Smith has offered his technical assistance, earning him a paragraph of his own this time around.

I couldn't be happier to work with the University of Iowa Press once again. My thanks to Karen Copp, Edie Roberts, Charlotte Wright, Prasenjit Gupta, Rhonda Wetjen, and to all of the interns. Special thanks to Holly Carver, director of the press, for listening to my pitch. My sincere gratitude for the tireless work of marketing and publicity guru (and bowler extraordinaire) Megan Scott.

This book absolutely could not have been put together without the help of the authors included in these pages. Time and again, they went above and beyond the call of duty, helping to secure permissions and offering suggestions. Their support made this anthology possible. If you like what you read here, please buy their books!

My father has always been there to assist with the grunt work of my career, such as helping me move across the country for one-year visiting appointments. He's that rare person who can be counted on to show up at a moment's notice.

My wife, Amy Knox Brown, consistently offers sound advice, and she is exceedingly patient with me whenever I start to panic, as I inevitably do with each project. My love to her.

# introduction

In the summer of 1999, the department chair at the University of Wisconsin at Madison asked me if I would like to teach a course titled "Voices of Humor in American Literature." I was about to finish teaching a three-week course on the American crime novel, which I had been asked to take over in the first week after the professor had fallen ill. The humor class, normally taught by that same professor, was to begin in three days. I'd never taught a "humor and literature" course before and I had never taken one as a student. I hadn't even read any of the books on this particular syllabus. Without hesitation, I gave the chair my answer. "Sure!" I said.

Needless to say, I had no idea what I was stepping into. I made a few changes right away—more group projects (admittedly, to lessen my burden) and more contemporary books (to capitalize on my own strengths). I used many of Walter Blair's classic books about humor in literature to guide my historical discussions, but since these books focused primarily on white writers, I had hoped to find some contemporary critical studies books on the role of humor in the works of minority writers. My plan was to use these critical studies as guides in selecting primary texts by minority writers, which I could then incorporate into the eight-week course. The evolution of my own disillusionment went like this: first, I looked for entire books on the subject of humor and the minority writer—none; then, I looked for essays in critical studies collections—none; next, I started asking other professors and writers if they could name some minority writers who used humor in their work—none; finally, I asked some of the local booksellers (often the best-read people around) if they could help me out. One bookseller offered three names: Sherman Alexie, Gish Jen, and Erika Lopez. Alexie and Jen were, in fact, the only writers I had already thought of, which left Erika Lopez as the sole writer whose work I didn't know. (Much later, someone reminded me of the work of Ishmael Reed [an obvious oversight!], Langston Hughes and his "Simple" stories, and Zora Neale Hurston, all writers who *should* have come to mind but for one reason or another didn't.)

As for humor anthologies, of which there are many, my findings weren't any more promising. In his useful essay "Teaching a Text-Based Humor Course," Donald Barlow Stauffer says, "Most humor anthologies I have seen (with the exception of [Roy Blount Jr.'s *Roy Blount's Book of Southern Humor*]) are virtually lily-white: they contain few, if any, writings by blacks, Native Americans, or other ethnic minorities" (235). In fact, since teaching that humor course, I have found only one anthology that is dedicated to the work of minority writers, Daryl Cumber Dance's *Honey, Hush!*, an amazingly comprehensive anthology of African American women's humor. Not surprisingly, Dance bemoans in *her* introduction the lack of critical attention given to her subject: "There are scores of treatments of women's humor (and these are rather recent): most of them say nothing about black women, and others give them short shrift" (xxix).

I couldn't interpret what my findings (or lack thereof) meant: Was I asking the wrong people, or were there only a handful of minority writers who used humor in their work, or were there minority writers who did, in fact, use humor but whose work wasn't getting published?

The answer to all three of these questions is, to some degree, *yes*.

Was I asking the wrong people? Since this anthology exists, the answer is clearly yes. To determine *why* the answer is yes is tricky, however, and we have to look at the answers in order to understand why I was asking the wrong people.

The next two questions, however, present a sort of riddle, because it's difficult to determine the logical cause and effect. The conundrum is this: Are these writers not getting published because there are only a handful of them, or are there only a handful that we know about because the others aren't getting published?

I can't provide empirical evidence for any of my conclusions—my conclusions are based on speculation, my experience editing this anthology, and what some of the writers in this book have told me—but I suspect the latter to be true, that the work is out there but not getting published. Lara Stapleton, a Filipina American writer, points a finger at the publishing world in her article "Liberating the Immigrant Novel." She defines the immigrant novel as a "work by people who are from, or who are the children from, non-European countries" (21) and she believes that editors, at both commercial houses and small presses, are looking for specific attributes in the immigrant novels that they acquire—namely, attributes that resemble an Amy Tan novel. Stapleton writes:

> Again and again, we are asked to tell the story of our childhood (not that that is a bad thing—being limited is a bad thing), our coming of age as foreigners in America. Often we are told our work is too ambitiously historical, or too postmodern in structure. Our novels should not be satire; we should not use too much irony. Our protagonists should be flawless. Victims are preferred as main characters. (22)

If there's truth in what Stapleton writes, then it would appear that publishers have developed a formula for the immigrant novel, and within that formula is little, if any, room for deviation, including the use of humor. If this is the case, we can hold the publishing world culpable for its narrow view of what should constitute "the immigrant novel," and for not considering other possibilities, other visions. Case closed.

Or can we? Is it *really* fair to blame the publishing world? On several occasions, I have placed "calls for submissions" for anthologies that I considered editing. For an anthology of stories on the subject of weddings—an anthology that was never published—I received about eight hundred submissions. For an anthology of short stories about the college experience, I received about five hundred submissions. For this anthology—humor by writers of color—I received fewer than a dozen submissions.

What does this tell us? The logical conclusion might be that not many writers of color use humor in their work. If this is the case, then how can we blame the publishing world for not publishing books that don't exist? After all, an editor is always limited by the submissions that he or she receives. On the other hand, if writers feel that the publishers aren't open to certain types of writing—and Stapleton's point that publishers want the next Amy Tan novel is a valid one—then wouldn't this discourage writers from taking risks and writing something that might be less marketable? One need look no further than the syllabi of most multicultural literature courses at universities across this country to see that the vast majority of required novels in those courses perfectly match the formula that Stapleton identifies, and since most writers these days are college educated, no one needs to spell out for them what's marketable and what's not.

Another possibility is that we are only now being introduced to a new generation of writers of color who find it easier than previous generations to incorporate humor into their material. Were writers of color from past generations who used humor in their work met with resistance? As any good humorist knows, humor can be a far more subversive and devastating tool than directness. In the introduction to her anthology *The Signet Book of American Humor*, Regina Barreca writes that "humor is gratifying in direct proportion to its rebelliousness" (xxi). She goes on to say that "all great humor, regardless of country of origin, is about risk and privilege," and that "nothing bothers an American humorist more than seeing people comfortable when they should be uncomfortable" (xxii). Barreca is writing about humorists in general. Now imagine the minority humorist of thirty, forty, fifty years ago, and try to imagine the reception that this humorist might have received from a predominantly white audience. In a country that didn't pass the Civil Rights Act until 1964, the minority writer of the twentieth century's first half who used humor—who, in Barreca's language, rebelled and made people uncomfortable—must surely have been at a greater risk, both personally and artistically, than the minority writer of today.

Consider, for instance, the comments of literary critic Jesse Bier. In his 1968 book *The Rise and Fall of American Humor*, Bier provides examples of what he calls "the more fearsome and bitter Negro humor," such as slave humor: "A black hen laid a white egg, and they hung her" (336). Bier then follows with examples of what he calls "objective humor": "the objective Negro comics can tell jokes on themselves which the rest of us wish not to tell; when God was cooking up the universe and was working on the world and human beings, he held up a Negro and said, 'Another burnt one!'" (337). He concludes by complimenting the then-contemporary African American humorist for moving away from the fearsome and bitter humor to one that self-mocks:

> Our fastest-rising minority group, the Negroes, are themselves our best and newest teachers of how to avoid the excesses of our blackest humor, all the more when that humor seems most certified by events. They teach the self-resistant tact we may still combine with objectivity in therapeutic comedy. (338)

In other words, it makes for better comedy when minority humorists make fun of themselves than when they use humor to skewer a social injustice. It's a win-win situation: it's therapeutic for "them" and it's funny to "us."

Bear in mind that *The Rise and Fall of American Humor* was published *post*– Civil Rights Act by a commercial publisher and that Bier spends *fewer than three pages* out of 506 on the subject of minority humor, half of those three pages being on Jewish humor. If this is any reflection of the times—the late sixties—one can just imagine the critical response to minority writers using "fearsome and bitter" humor in the *pre*– Civil Rights Act era.

The 1960s were a cusp, and to find a good example of a minority humorist's career on that cusp we need to turn from literature to the performing arts. One of the most interesting careers to examine is comedian Richard Pryor's. In his essay "Now's the Time: The Richard Pryor Phenomenon and the Triumph of Black Culture," Siva Vaidhyanathan writes the following:

> Before 1969, Pryor—especially on television—was doing what Pryor called "that Cosby shit." His material, mostly innocuous stories with some racial tinge, was generally reheated, "safe" material. When Pryor returned to Los Angeles from Berkeley in 1970, he was angry, he was sexual, he was scary, and he was almost instantly successful. (44)

Vaidhyanathan believes that by 1970 American culture craved "rebelliousness, courage, creativity, and soul," the result of which was white America's interest in black culture, particularly in terms of black music and the rising popularity of black sports figures (45). This was exactly the sort of crossover appeal that Richard Pryor craved, and by the mid-1970s he had achieved his goal of becoming one of the most popular performers in the country. But something curious had happened along the way. There were suddenly two distinctly different Pryors: the volatile stand-up comedian versus the Hollywood actor.

Anyone who followed Richard Pryor's career in the seventies and eighties, which I did as a child and then as a teenager, could see the dichotomy between these two Pryors. In his stand-up acts, Pryor had free reign to say and do what he pleased, and the fuel of his anger was what ignited the humor. No doubt his act, which included impersonations of uptight whites, would have been labeled by critic Jesse Bier as "fearsome and bitter Negro humor," and yet by the 1970s whites as well as blacks had embraced Richard Pryor and his brand of humor.

The Richard Pryor of Hollywood movies, on the other hand, was often reduced to "mugging for the cameras," as Vaidhyanathan puts it. He wasn't the angry, sexual, or scary persona of his stand-up act. He became, in essence, Bier's ideal "objective Negro" comic who could tell jokes on himself. And yet, according to writer Ishmael Reed, who was Richard Pryor's friend in the early days of his career, it was Hollywood that ruined Pryor:

> Richard should have stayed in Berkeley. Free speech was invented in Berkeley. I don't think Hollywood served him too well. The circle he was running around with here [in Berkeley] was very positive to him. Hollywood just ruined him. What was that thing he did with Jackie Gleason? *The Toy*? What was that shit? (Vaidhyanathan 44)

Pryor's career is emblematic of what often happens to a groundbreaking, innovative talent once corporate America gets hold of him or her. Hollywood, like the New York publishing world, was (and is) run, by and large, by whites, and certainly in the 1970s and the early 1980s, these industries catered primarily to white audiences. I'm not suggesting that the film giants and the publishing giants don't still cater to white America, but at some point both industries seemed to become aware that nonwhite actors and writers could be marketable as well. Along with this understanding was the possibility of new viable markets—that is, audiences that weren't necessarily all white. And once something is deemed marketable, doors suddenly fly open and trends start to develop. This was certainly the case with Amy Tan. After the success of Tan's *The Joy Luck Club*, publishers appeared to be climbing over each other to find the next "hot" Asian American writer.

Intellectual cultural revolutions can bring about only so much change. In order to make significant alterations to a culture, there must be a viable market for the product so that the big guns—i.e., Hollywood or New York publishing—can pump money into advertising it, at which point the product will enter the mainstream and have an effect on the culture as a whole. This is a cynical observation, but even more cynical is the conclusion drawn from the story of Richard Pryor's career in Hollywood, a career that, to some minds, undermined much of his achievement as a culturally significant comic. Hollywood executives are from the dominant culture, and if the viable market is also the dominant culture, we can't have anything that's too angry, too sexual, or too scary if it's *not* from the dominant culture. Hollywood is far more likely to serve up for us Bier's "objective Negro humor" than his "fearsome and bitter Negro humor." After all, what fun would it be for us, the mass consumer, if the humor strikes a nerve?

As for trends in publishing, we've witnessed in these past two decades a growing interest in multicultural writing, no doubt because a viable market has been identified. And I suspect that the reason we haven't seen much humor in multicultural writing isn't because writers aren't writing it, but rather because the humor is still perceived, by the higher-ups, to be too angry, too sexual, and too scary, and because the viable market is still predominantly white. What Regina Barreca says about her own anthology, *The Signet Book of American Humor*, applies to *Humor Me* as well: "If most of the humor in this volume doesn't bother you, if it doesn't disturb you just a little bit, you're missing the point and ducking the very real punch in the punchline" (xxii). The major difference with *Humor Me* is that the punch is more likely to be coming from across the border of race, which sometimes stings just a bit more.

One thing I learned from teaching that humor course is that you can't *make* someone find something funny that they otherwise wouldn't find funny. Before the discussion of each assigned book, I would ask the simple and unscholarly question, "Who found this funny?" Those who didn't find a particular book funny would remain unconvinced for the duration of the discussion. Often, they couldn't fathom why I had put the book on the syllabus. The polls sometimes showed curious results. A collection of stories by Lorrie Moore split along gender lines: women in the class found it funny; men, for the most part, didn't. Also, the darker the humor I assigned, the fewer the people who found it funny. What fared best was humor that was situational with strong comic characters. John Kennedy Toole's *A Confederacy of Dunces* was the victor, narrowly squeaking by Mark Twain's *The Adventures of Huckleberry Finn*.

It's one thing to teach the criteria of modes of humor; it's another thing to get people to acknowledge that there might actually *be* humor in something they themselves do not find funny. One's sense of humor seems so ingrained in one's personality as to appear almost genetic. I'm sure that a number of factors come into play in the development of one's sense of humor, but we do seem to acquire a distinct sense of humor at a very early age, and many people I've known from childhood have maintained a consistent sensibility through adulthood. Granted, their sense of humor has become more sophisticated, but the same *sorts* of humor still appeal to them.

Editing an anthology of humor, therefore, is a dangerous endeavor—the danger being that one reader may not find anything funny in it at all. It would be easy for me to call this imaginary reader a sourpuss and leave it at that, but I know better. Even though I've attempted to choose works by writers who use different sorts of humor, I'm sure that my tastes, however concealed, will become evident as one reads the book.

One can't overlook the various factors that will make one person laugh at a particular piece while another scratches his or her head. It's no surprise that what one generation finds funny, another generation may not. Irony certainly has a broader appeal to younger readers than to, say, readers from my parents' generation, men and women who were kids during the Depression. We are now mired in a world of irony in a way that people of that generation were not, and this saturation during our upbringing must surely shape our sensibilities. (If you doubt this, show Erika Lopez's graphic narrative to a group of octogenarians and gauge their reactions.)

Humor that uses popular culture creates yet another generational gap. A story such as Michele Serros's "I Know What You Did Last Summer," which is about a Lollapalooza road poet during the era of grunge, may cause a few readers who missed that particular phenomenon to feel out of the cultural loop.

Early American humor was often regional in nature, and although America has become more homogeneous, one might still find a divide between urban and rural humor. This divide may come down to what concerns us on a daily basis: going to trendy nightclubs vs. doing business at the local feed store. We tend to find more humor in those subjects to which we can relate. If we can empathize on a personal level with the plight of the narrator, then we're likely to find more humor in the situation, so long as there is truth in the story and accuracy in the details.

Education is another factor. If one facet of education is to broaden one's base of knowledge, then it stands to reason that the broader our knowledge, the more likely it is that our humor will be more finely tuned. If we're reading a parody of a literary work, we're more likely to find the parody funny if we've read the literary work that's being parodied. In this way, our sense of humor becomes more sophisticated, which isn't to say that one who finds the Three Stooges funny wouldn't find them less funny as he or she receives more education. In fact, we may find it funnier because we've become more attuned to the movies' *surreal* characteristics (though I'll confess, as a Stooges fan, I may be stretching my argument a bit here).

Race may be another contributing factor in much the same way that region may define what's funny; if the particulars of an experience are foreign to the reader, the reader may not understand what's funny and what's not. Most of the humor in this anthology that deals with race issues doesn't rely on a reader's empathy for having gone through that same experience; however, I suspect that readers will find funnier those pieces with which they *can* empathize.

Since the overarching theme of this book—humor—is so subjective, it might be worthwhile for me to provide a peek at my agendas in putting this book together. *Humor Me* is not a collection of work by humorists. Rather, humor plays a role in each piece, but that role varies, often dramatically, from one author to the next. The sort of overt humor that you'll find in Jim Northrup's play *Shinnob Jep*, a parody of the game show *Jeopardy!*, is vastly different from the more subdued humor in Paisley Rekdal's essay about traveling to Taipei with her mother.

Race is not the central theme of this book. *Humor Me* is a showcase for writers of color who use humor in their work, regardless of subject matter. That said, race does play a central role in several pieces (race is at the heart of Sherman Alexie's short story "Assimilation" and his essay "White Men Can't Drum"), but it barely creeps into other works (Sandra Tsing Loh's essay "Daddy Dearest" is really more about embarrassing family members than race, though race is present), and in some pieces it's not there at all (see Erika Lopez's graphic story "Draining Like a Dead Chicken"). The dominant themes in this book are the dominant themes one might find in any general interest anthology: family, sex, love, and race—or a combination of two or more of these.

*Humor Me* is not a historical look at humor by writers of color, nor is it meant to be comprehensive in scope. It isn't even all-inclusive, in terms of race, despite my best efforts. *Humor Me* is a sampling, a taste, of what's out there. Included are contemporary writers, some of whom are more established than others. You'll find Charles Johnson and Lucille Clifton alongside newcomers Aimee Nezhukumatathil and Daniel Chacón. As with any sampler, I encourage you to seek out the books by those authors whose work you especially enjoy.

Every anthology editor has limitations—namely, space (no editor can include everything that he or she would like to include) and selection (fees to reprint previously published material are sometimes more than my entire budget). There is also the limitation of the editor's knowledge, a limitation the depths of which I'm fearful to tread. What, after all, are my qualifications for editing this book? I've edited two previous anthologies; I taught the aforementioned humor course (albeit as a last-minute, unqualified replacement); I'm a fiction writer who uses humor in his work; and I've been teaching creative writing and literature for a dozen years. So what's the problem? For starters, I'm not a scholar of humor in literature (though my first unpublished book, written when I was twelve, was about comedy teams). Also, I am not a writer of color. I'm a white guy. There's no getting around this fact. Put my name in a small font and leave my photo off the book, but I'm still a white guy editing an anthology of works by writers of color. I mention this only so that you, the reader, can further put the selection process into perspective, factoring in my race as a variable. What effect does this have on the book? I don't know. Several selections were recommended to me by other authors in this book, so my role, in many instances, was that of a middleman. (I should note that the authors in this book have been extraordinarily supportive of this project and that their active participation in helping me with it gives me hope that I haven't screwed up too terribly, although it's always possible that these authors are misguided and that I have screwed up. But no: surely that's not the case.) In other instances, editors at presses that publish exclusively minority writers made recommendations, some of which I used. Perhaps a case can be made that what I've done is akin to what I described earlier—that someone from the dominant culture has made decisions about what works by minority artists should be published, thereby controlling what gets seen and read. My only defense is that my inspiration for this particular book came out of my frustrations while teaching that humor course. What I've attempted to do is to assemble the book that I was searching for that semester, the book I couldn't find.

Upon hearing about this project, one African American scholar asked me, smiling, "So, what do those of us on the other side of the racial divide have to laugh about?" The question was part serious, part joshing, but I think it gets to the heart of this anthology and, more generally, to the nature of humor itself. Daryl Cumber Dance says, "The formula for humor is said to be tragedy plus time, or pain plus time" (xxi). If this is true, there probably isn't much to laugh about in the "tragedy" or "pain" part of this equation; but it's what these writers *do* with tragedy and pain, how they transform it through the filter of satire or parody or farce, that turns their raw subjects into an impressive and often hilarious work of art.

## works cited

Barreca, Regina, ed. *The Signet Book of American Humor*. New York: Signet, 1999.

Bier, Jesse. *The Rise and Fall of American Humor*. New York: Holt, Rinehart and Winston, 1968.

Blount, Roy, Jr., ed. *Roy Blount's Book of Southern Humor*. New York: W. W. Norton, 1994.

Dance, Daryl Cumber, ed. *Honey Hush! An Anthology of African American Women's Humor*. New York: Norton, 1998.

Stapleton, Lara. "Liberating the Immigrant Novel." *Poets & Writers*, Jan/Feb 2001: 21–24.

Stauffer, Donald Barlow. "Teaching a Text-Based Humor Course: 'You can't get there from here, stranger.'" In *New Directions in American Humor*, ed. David E. E. Sloane. Tuscaloosa: University of Alabama Press, 1998, 233–44.

Vaidhyanathan, Siva. "Now's the Time: The Richard Pryor Phenomenon and the Triumph of Black Culture." In *New Directions in American Humor*, ed. David E. E. Sloane. Tuscaloosa: University of Alabama Press, 1998, 40–50.

# PART ONE

# fiction

# Assimilation

## SHERMAN ALEXIE

Regarding love, marriage, and sex, both Shakespeare and Sitting Bull knew the only truth: treaties get broken. Therefore, Mary Lynn wanted to have sex with any man other than her husband. For the first time in her life, she wanted to go to bed with an Indian man only because he was Indian. She was a Coeur d'Alene Indian married to a white man; she was a wife who wanted to have sex with an indigenous stranger. She didn't care about the stranger's job or his hobbies, or whether he was due for a Cost of Living raise, or owned ten thousand miles of model railroad track. She didn't care if he was handsome or ugly, mostly because she wasn't sure exactly what those terms meant anymore and how much relevance they truly had when it came to choosing sexual partners. Oh, she'd married a very handsome man, there was no doubt about that, and she was still attracted to her husband, to his long, graceful fingers, to his arrogance and utter lack of fear in social situations—he'd say anything to anybody—but lately, she'd been forced to concentrate too hard when making love to him. If she didn't focus completely on him, on the smallest details of his body, then she would drift away from the bed and float around the room like a bored angel. Of course, all this made her feel like a failure, especially since it seemed that her husband had yet to notice her growing disinterest. She wanted to be a good lover, wife, and partner, but she'd obviously developed some form of sexual dyslexia or had picked up a mutant, contagious, and erotic strain of Attention Deficit Disorder. She felt baffled by the complications of sex. She haunted the aisles of bookstores and desperately paged through every book in the self-help section and studied every diagram and chart in the human sensuality encyclopedias. She wanted answers. She wanted to feel it again, whatever *it* was.

A few summers ago, during Crow Fair, Mary Lynn had been standing in a Montana supermarket, in the produce aisle, when a homely white woman, her spiky blond hair still wet from a trailer-house shower, walked by in a white T-shirt and blue jeans, and though Mary Lynn was straight—having politely declined all three lesbian overtures thrown at her in her life—she'd felt a warm breeze pass through her DNA in that ugly woman's wake, and had briefly wanted to knock her to the linoleum and do beautiful things to her. Mary Lynn had never before felt such lust—in Montana, of all places, for a white woman who was functionally illiterate and underemployed! — and had not since felt that sensually about any other woman or man.

Who could explain such things, these vagaries of love? There were many people who would blame Mary Lynn's unhappiness, her dissatisfaction, on her ethnicity. God, she thought, how simple and earnest was that particular bit of psychotherapy! Yes, she was most certainly a Coeur d'Alene—she'd grown up on the rez, had been very happy during her time there, and had left without serious regrets or full-time enemies—but that wasn't the only way to define her. She wished that she could be called Coeur d'Alene as a description, rather than as an excuse, reasons, prescription, placebo, prediction, or diminutive. She only wanted to be understood as eccentric and complicated!

Her most cherished eccentricity: when she was feeling her most lonely, she'd put one of the Big Mom Singers's powwow CDs on the stereo *(I'm not afraid of death, hey, ya, hey, death is my cousin, hey, ya, ha, ha)* and read from Emily Dickinson's poetry *(Because I could not stop for Death— / He kindly stopped for me—).*

Her most important complication: she was a woman in a turbulent marriage that was threatening to go bad, or had gone bad and might get worse.

Yes, she was a Coeur d'Alene woman, passionately and dispassionately, who wanted to cheat on her white husband because he was white. She wanted to find an anonymous lover, an Indian man who would fade away into the crowd when she was done with him, a man whose face could appear on the back of her milk carton. She didn't care if he was the kind of man who knew the punch lines to everybody's dirty jokes, or if he was the kind of man who read Zane Grey before he went to sleep, or if he was both of those men simultaneously. She simply wanted to find the darkest Indian in Seattle—the man with the greatest amount of melanin—and get naked with him in a cheap motel room. Therefore, she walked up to a flabby Lummi Indian man in a coffee shop and asked him to make love to her.

"Now," she said. "Before I change my mind."

He hesitated for a brief moment, wondering why he was the chosen one, and then took her by the hand. He decided to believe he was a handsome man.

"Don't you want to know my name?" he asked before she put her hand over his mouth.

"Don't talk to me," she said. "Don't say one word. Just take me to the closest motel and fuck me."

The obscenity bothered her. It felt staged, forced, as if she were an actress in a three-in-the-morning cable-television movie. But she was acting, wasn't she? She was not an adulteress, was she?

Why exactly did she want to have sex with an Indian stranger? She told herself it was because of pessimism, existentialism, even nihilism, but those reasons—*those words*—were a function of her vocabulary and not of her motivations. If forced to admit the truth, or some version of the truth, she'd testify she was about to go to bed with an Indian stranger because she wanted to know how it would feel. After all, she'd slept with a white stranger in her life, so why not include a Native American? Why not practice a carnal form of affirmative action? By God, her infidelity was a political act! Rebellion, resistance, revolution!

In the motel room, Mary Lynn made the Indian take off his clothes first. Thirty pounds overweight, with purple scars crisscrossing his pale chest and belly, he trembled as he undressed. He wore a wedding ring on his right hand. She knew that some Europeans wore their wedding bands on the right hand—so maybe this Indian was married to a French woman—but Mary Lynn also knew that some divorced Americans wore rings on their right hands as symbols of pain, of mourning. Mary Lynn didn't care if he was married or not, or whether he shared custody of the sons and daughters, or whether he had any children at all. She was grateful that he was plain and desperate and lonely.

Mary Lynn stepped close to him, took his hand, and slid his thumb into her mouth. She sucked on it and felt ridiculous. His skin was salty and oily, the taste of a working man. She closed her eyes and thought about her husband, a professional who had his shirts laundered. In one hour, he was going to meet her at a new downtown restaurant.

She walked a slow, tight circle around the Indian. She stood behind him, reached around his thick waist, and held his erect penis. He moaned and she decided that she hated him. She decided to hate all men. Hate, hate, hate, she thought, and then let her hate go.

She was lovely and intelligent, and had grown up with Indian women who were more lovely and more intelligent, but who also had far less ambition and mendacity. She'd once read in a book, perhaps by Primo Levi or Elie Wiesel, that the survivors of the Nazi death camps were the Jews who lied, cheated, murdered, stole, and subverted. You must remember, said Levi or Wiesel, that the best of us did not survive the camps. Mary Lynn felt the same way about the reservation. Before she'd turned ten, she'd attended the funerals of seventeen good women—the best of the Coeur d'Alenes— and had read about the deaths of eighteen more good women since she'd left the rez. But what about the Coeur d'Alene men—those liars, cheats, and thieves—who'd survived, even thrived? Mary Lynn wanted nothing to do with them, then or now. As a teenager, she'd dated only white boys. As an adult, she'd dated only white men. God, she hated to admit it, but white men—her teachers, coaches, bosses, and lovers—had always been more dependable than the Indian men in her life. White men had rarely disappointed her, but they'd never surprised her either. White men were neutral, she thought, just like Belgium! And when has Belgium ever been sexy? When has Belgium caused a grown woman to shake with fear and guilt? She didn't want to feel Belgium; she wanted to feel dangerous.

In the cheap motel room, Mary Lynn breathed deeply. The Indian smelled of old sweat and a shirt worn twice before washing. She ran her finger along the ugly scars on his belly and chest. She wanted to know the scars' creation story—she hoped this Indian man was a warrior with a history of knife fighting—but she feared he was only carrying the transplanted heart and lungs of another man. She pushed him onto the bed, onto the scratchy comforter. She'd once read that scientists had examined a hotel-room comforter and discovered four hundred and thirty-two different samples of sperm. God, she thought, those scientists obviously had too much time on their hands and, in the end, had failed to ask the most important questions: Who left the samples? Spouses, strangers? Were these exchanges of money, tenderness, disease? Was there love?

"This has to be quick," she said to the stranger beside her.

Jeremiah, her husband, was already angry when Mary Lynn arrived thirty minutes late at the restaurant and he nearly lost all of his self-control when they were asked to wait for the next available table. He often raged at strangers, though he was incredibly patient and kind with their four children. Mary Lynn had seen that kind of rage in other white men when their wishes and desires were ignored. At ball games, in parking lots, and especially in airports, white men demanded to receive the privileges whose very existence they denied. White men could be so predictable, thought Mary Lynn. She thought: O, Jeremiah! O, season ticket holder! O, monthly parker! O, frequent flyer! She dreamed of him out there, sitting in the airplane with eighty-seven other white men wearing their second-best suits, all of them traveling toward small rooms in the Ramadas, Radissons, and sometimes the Hyatts, where they all separately watched the same pay-per-view porno that showed everything except penetration. What's the point of porno without graphic penetration? Mary Lynn knew it only made these lonely men feel all that more lonely. And didn't they deserve better, these white salesmen and middle managers, these twenty-first-century Willie Lomans, who only wanted to be better men than their fathers had been? Of course, thought Mary Lynn, these sons definitely deserved better—they were smarter and more tender and generous than all previous generations of white American men—but they'd never receive their just rewards, and thus their anger was justified and banal.

"Calm down," Mary Lynn said to her husband as he continued to rage at the restaurant hostess.

Mary Lynn said those two words to him more often in their marriage than any other combination of words.

"It could be twenty, thirty minutes," said the hostess. "Maybe longer."

"We'll wait outside," said Jeremiah. He breathed deeply, remembering some mantra that his therapist had taught him.

Mary Lynn's mantra: I cheated on my husband, I cheated on my husband.

"We'll call your name," said the hostess, a white woman who was tired of men no matter what their color. "When."

Their backs pressed against the brick wall, their feet crossed on the sidewalk, on a warm Seattle evening, Mary Lynn and Jeremiah smoked faux cigarettes filled with some foul-tasting, overwhelmingly organic herb substance. For years they had smoked unfiltered Camels, but had quit after all four of their parents had simultaneously suffered through at least one form of cancer. Mary Lynn had called them the Mormon Tabernacle Goddamn Cancer Choir, though none of them was Mormon and all of them were altos. With and without grace, they had all survived the radiation, chemo-therapy, and in-hospital cable-television bingo games, with their bodies reasonably intact, only to resume their previously self-destructive habits. After so many nights spent in hospital corridors, waiting rooms, and armchairs, Mary Lynn and Jeremiah hated doctors, all doctors, even ones on television, especially ones on television. United in their obsessive hatred, Mary Lynn and Jeremiah resorted to taking vitamins, eating free-range chicken, and smoking cigarettes rolled together and marketed by six odoriferous white liberals in Northern California.

As they waited for a table, Mary Lynn and Jeremiah watched dozens of people arrive and get seated immediately.

"I bet they don't have reservations," he said.

"I hate these cigarettes," she said.

"Why do you keep buying them?"

"Because the cashier at the health-food store is cute."

"You're shallow."

"Like a mud puddle."

Mary Lynn hated going out on weeknights. She hated driving into the city. She hated waiting for a table. Standing outside the downtown restaurant, desperate to hear their names, she decided to hate Jeremiah for a few seconds. Hate, hate, hate, she thought, and then she let her hate go. She wondered if she smelled like sex, like indigenous sex, and if a white man could recognize the scent of an enemy. She'd showered, but the water pressure had been weak and the soap bar too small.

"Let's go someplace else," she said.

"No. Five seconds after we leave, they'll call our names."

"But we won't know they called our names."

"But I'll feel it."

"It must be difficult to be psychic and insecure."

"I knew you were going to say that."

Clad in leather jackets and black jeans, standing inches apart but never quite touching, both handsome to the point of distraction, smoking crappy cigarettes that appeared to be real cigarettes, they could have been the subjects of a Schultz photograph or a Runnette poem.

The title of the photograph: "Infidelity."

The title of the poem: "More Infidelity."

Jeremiah's virtue was reasonably intact, though he'd recently been involved in a flirtatious near-affair with a coworker. At the crucial moment, when the last button was about to be unbuttoned, when consummation was just a fingertip away, Jeremiah had pushed his potential lover away and said I can't, I just can't, I love my marriage. He didn't admit to love for his spouse, partner, wife. No, he confessed his love for marriage, for the blessed union, for the legal document, for the shared mortgage payments, and for their four children.

Mary Lynn wondered what would happen if she grew pregnant with the Lummi's baby. Would this full-blood baby look more Indian than her half-blood sons and daughters?

"Don't they know who I am?" she asked her husband as they waited outside the downtown restaurant. She wasn't pregnant; there would be no paternity tests, no revealing of great secrets. His secret: he was still in love with a white woman from high school he hadn't seen in decades. What Mary Lynn knew: he was truly in love with the idea of a white woman from a mythical high school, with a prom queen named *If Only* or a homecoming princess named *My Life Could Have Been Different*.

"I'm sure they know who you are," he said. "That's why we're on the wait list. Otherwise, we'd be heading for McDonald's or Denny's."

"Your kinds of places."

"Dependable. The Big Mac you eat in Hong Kong or Des Moines tastes just like the Big Mac in Seattle."

"Sounds like colonialism to me."

"Colonialism ain't all bad."

"Put that on a bumper sticker."

This place was called Tan Tan, though it would soon be trendy enough to go by a nickname: Tan's. Maybe Tan's would become T's, and then T's would be identified only by a slight turn of the head or a certain widening of the eyes. After that, the downhill slide in reputation would be inevitable, whether or not the culinary content and quality of the restaurant remained exactly the same or improved. As it was, Tan Tan was a pan-Asian restaurant whose ownership and chefs—head, sauce, and line—were white, though most of the wait staff appeared to be one form of Asian or another.

"Don't you hate it?" Jeremiah asked. "When they have Chinese waiters in sushi joints? Or Korean dishwashers in a Thai noodle house?"

"I hadn't really thought about it," she said.

"No, think about it, these restaurants, these Asian restaurants, they hire Asians indiscriminately because they think white people won't be able to tell the difference."

"White people can't tell the difference."

"I can."

"Hey, Geronimo, you've been hanging around Indians too long to be white."

"Fucking an Indian doesn't make me Indian."

"So, that's what we're doing now? Fucking?"

"You have a problem with fucking?"

"No, not with the act itself, but I do have a problem with your sexual thesaurus."

Mary Lynn and Jeremiah had met in college, when they were still called Mary and Jerry. After sleeping together for the first time, after her first orgasm and his third, Mary had turned to Jerry and said, with absolute seriousness: If this thing is going to last, we have to stop the end rhyme. She had majored in Milton and Blake. He'd been a chemical engineer since the age of seven, with the degree being only a matter of formality, so he'd had plenty of time to wonder how an Indian from the reservation could be so smart. He still wondered how it had happened, though he'd never had the courage to ask her.

Now, a little more than two decades after graduating with a useless degree, Mary Lynn worked at Microsoft for a man named Dickinson. Jeremiah didn't know his first name, though he hoped it wasn't Emery, and had never met the guy, and didn't care if he ever did. Mary Lynn's job title and responsibilities were vague, so vague that Jeremiah had never asked her to elaborate. She often worked sixty-hour weeks and he didn't want to reward that behavior by expressing an interest in what specific tasks she performed for Bill Gates.

Waiting outside Tan Tan, he and she could smell ginger, burned rice, beer.

"Are they ever going to seat us?" she asked.

"Yeah, don't they know who you are?"

"I hear this place discriminates against white people."

"Really?"

"Yeah, I heard once, these lawyers, bunch of white guys in Nordstrom's suits, had to wait, like, two hours for a table."

"Were those billable hours?"

"It's getting hard for a white guy to find a place to eat."

"Damn affirmative action is what it is."

Their first child had been an accident, the result of a broken condom and a missed birth control pill. They named her Antonya, Toni for short. The second and third children, Robert and Michael, had been on purpose, and the fourth, Ariel, came after Mary Lynn thought she could no longer get pregnant.

Toni was fourteen, immature for her age, quite beautiful and narcissistic, with her translucent skin, her long blond hair, and eight-ball eyes. Botticelli eyes, she bragged after taking an Introduction to Art class. She never bothered to tell anybody she was Indian, mostly because nobody asked.

Jeremiah was quite sure that his daughter, his Antonya, had lost her virginity to the pimply quarterback of the junior-varsity football team. He found the thought of his daughter's adolescent sexuality both curious and disturbing. Above all else, he believed that she was far too special to sleep with a cliché, let alone a junior-varsity cliché.

Three months out of every year, Robert and Michael were the same age. Currently, they were both eleven. Dark-skinned, with their mother's black hair, strong jawline, and endless nose, they looked Indian, very Indian. Robert, who had refused to be called anything other than Robert, was the smart boy, a math prodigy, while Mikey was the basketball player.

When Mary Lynn's parents called from the reservation, they always asked after the boys, always invited the boys out for the weekend, the holidays, and the summer, and always sent the boys more elaborate gifts than they sent the two girls.

When Jeremiah had pointed out this discrepancy to Mary Lynn, she had readily agreed, but had made it clear that his parents also paid more attention to the boys. Jeremiah never mentioned it again, but had silently vowed to love the girls a little more than he loved the boys.

As if love were a thing that could be quantified, he thought.

He asked himself: What if I love the girls more because they look more like me, because they look more white than the boys?

Towheaded Ariel was two, and the clay of her personality was just beginning to harden, but she was certainly petulant and funny as hell, with the ability to sleep in sixteen-hour marathons that made her parents very nervous. She seemed to exist in her own world, enough so that she was periodically monitored for incipient autism. She treated her siblings as if they somehow bored her, and was the kind of kid who could stay alone in her crib for hours, amusing herself with all sorts of personal games and imaginary friends.

Mary Lynn insisted that her youngest daughter was going to be an artist, but Jeremiah didn't understand the child, and despite the fact that he was her father and forty-three years older, he felt inferior to Ariel.

He wondered if his wife was ever going to leave him because he was white.

When Tan Tan's doors swung open, laughter and smoke rolled out together.

"You got another cigarette?" he asked.

"Quit calling them cigarettes. They're not cigarettes. They're more like rose bushes. Hell, they're more like the shit that rose bushes grow in."

"You think we're going to get a table?"

"By the time we get a table, this place is going to be very unpopular."

"Do you want to leave?"

"Do you?"

"If you do."

"We told the baby-sitter we'd be home by ten."

They both wished that Toni were responsible enough to baby-sit her siblings, rather than needing to be sat along with them.

"What time is it?" she asked.

"Nine."

"Let's go home."

Last Christmas, when the kids had been splayed out all over the living room, buried to their shoulders in wrapping paper and expensive toys, Mary Lynn had studied her children's features, had recognized most of her face in her sons' faces and very little of it in her daughters', and had decided, quite facetiously, that the genetic score was tied.

We should have another kid, she'd said to Jeremiah, so we'll know if this is a white family or an Indian family.

It's a family family, he'd said, without a trace of humor.

Only a white guy would say that, she'd said.

Well, he'd said, you married a white guy.

The space between them had grown very cold at that moment, in that silence, and perhaps one or both of them might have said something truly destructive, but Ariel had started crying then, for no obvious reason, relieving both parents of the responsibility of finishing that particular conversation. During the course of their relationship, Mary Lynn and Jeremiah had often discussed race as a concept, as a foreign country they occasionally visited, or as an enemy that existed outside their house, as a destructive force they could fight against as a couple, as a family. But race was also a constant presence, a houseguest and permanent tenant who crept around all the rooms in their shared lives, opening drawers, stealing utensils and small articles of clothing, changing the temperature.

Before he'd married Mary Lynn, Jeremiah had always believed there was too much talk of race, that white people were all too willing to be racist and that brown people were just as willing and just as racist. As a rational scientist, he'd known that race was primarily a social construct, illusionary, but as the husband of an Indian woman and the father of Indian children, he'd since learned that race, whatever its construction, was real. Now, there were plenty of white people who wanted to eliminate the idea of race, to cast it aside as an unwanted invention, but it was far too late for that. If white people are the mad scientists who created race, thought Jeremiah, then we created race so we could enslave black people and kill Indians, and now race has become the Frankenstein monster that has grown beyond our control. Though he'd once been willfully blind, Jeremiah had learned how to recognize that monster in the faces of whites and Indians and in their eyes.

Long ago, Jeremiah and Mary Lynn had both decided to challenge those who stared by staring back, by flinging each other against walls and tongue-kissing with pornographic élan.

Long ago, they'd both decided to respond to any questions of why, how, what, who, or when by simply stating: Love is Love. They knew it was romantic bullshit, a simpleminded answer only satisfying for simpleminded people, but it was the best available defense.

Listen, Mary Lynn had once said to Jeremiah, asking somebody why they fall in love is like asking somebody why they believe in God.

You start asking questions like that, she had added, and you're either going to start a war or you're going to hear folk music.

You think too much, Jeremiah had said, rolling over and falling asleep.

Then, in the dark, as Jeremiah slept, Mary Lynn had masturbated while fantasizing about an Indian man with sun-dance scars on his chest.

After they left Tan Tan, they drove a sensible and indigenous Ford Taurus over the 520 bridge, back toward their house in Kirkland, a five-bedroom rancher only ten blocks away from the Microsoft campus. Mary Lynn walked to work. That made her feel privileged. She estimated there were twenty-two American Indians who had ever felt even a moment of privilege.

"We still have to eat," she said as she drove across the bridge. She felt strange. She wondered if she was ever going to feel normal again.

"How about Taco Bell drive-thru?" he asked.

"You devil, you're trying to get into my pants, aren't you?"

Impulsively, he dropped his head into her lap and pressed his lips against her black-jeaned crotch. She yelped and pushed him away. She wondered if he could smell her, if he could smell the Lummi Indian. Maybe he could, but he seemed to interpret it as something different, as something meant for him, as he pushed his head into her lap again. What was she supposed to do? She decided to laugh, so she did laugh as she pushed his face against her pubic bone. She loved the man for reasons she could not always explain. She closed her eyes, drove in that darkness, and felt dangerous.

Halfway across the bridge, Mary Lynn slammed on the brakes, not because she'd seen anything—her eyes were still closed—but because she'd felt something. The car skidded to a stop just inches from the bumper of a truck that had just missed sliding into the row of cars stopped ahead of it.

"What the hell is going on?" Jeremiah asked as he lifted his head from her lap.

"Traffic jam."

"Jesus, we'll never make it home by ten. We better call."

"The cell phone is in the glove."

Jeremiah dialed the home number but received only a busy signal.

"Toni must be talking to her boyfriend," she said.

"I don't like him."

"He doesn't like you."

"What the hell is going on? Why aren't we moving?"

"I don't know. Why don't you go check?" Jeremiah climbed out of the car.

"I was kidding," she said as he closed the door behind him. He walked up to the window of the truck ahead of him.

"You know what's going on?" Jeremiah asked the truck driver.

"Nope."

Jeremiah walked farther down the bridge. He wondered if there was a disabled car ahead, what the radio liked to call a "blocking accident." There was also the more serious "injury accident" and the deadly "accident with fatality involved." He had to drive this bridge ten times a week. The commute. White men had invented the commute, had deepened its meaning, had diversified its complications, and now spent most of the time trying to shorten it, reduce it, lessen it.

In the car, Mary Lynn wondered why Jeremiah always found it necessary to insert himself into every situation. He continually moved from the passive to the active. The man was kinetic. She wondered if it was a white thing. Possibly. But more likely, it was a Jeremiah thing. She remembered Mikey's third-grade-class's school play, an edited version of *Hamlet*. Jeremiah had walked onto the stage to help his son drag the unconscious Polonius, who had merely been clubbed over the head rather than stabbed to death, from the stage. Mortally embarrassed, Mikey had cried himself to sleep that night, positive that he was going to be an elementary-school pariah, while Jeremiah vainly tried to explain to the rest of the family why he had acted so impulsively.

I was just trying to be a good father, he had said.

Mary Lynn watched Jeremiah walk farther down the bridge. He was just a shadow, a silhouette. She was slapped by the brief, irrational fear that he would never return.

Husband, come back to me, she thought, and I will confess.

Impatient drivers honked their horns. Mary Lynn joined them. She hoped Jeremiah would recognize the specific sound of their horn and return to the car.

Listen to me, listen to me, listen to me, she thought as she pounded the steering wheel.

Jeremiah heard their car horn, but only as one note in the symphony of noise playing on the bridge. He walked through that noise, through an ever-increasing amount of noise, until he pushed through a sudden crowd of people and found himself witnessing a suicide.

Illuminated by headlights, the jumper was a white woman, pretty, wearing a sundress and good shoes. Jeremiah could see that much as she stood on the bridge railing, forty feet above the cold water.

He could hear sirens approaching from both sides of the bridge, but they would never make it through the traffic in time to save this woman.

The jumper was screaming somebody's name.

Jeremiah stepped closer, wanting to hear the name, wanting to have that information so that he could use it later. To what use, he didn't know, but he knew that name had value, importance. That name, the owner of that name, was the reason why the jumper stood on the bridge.

"Aaron," she said. The jumper screamed, "Aaron."

In the car, Mary Lynn could not see either Jeremiah or the jumper, but she could see dozens of drivers leaving their cars and running ahead.

She was suddenly and impossibly sure that her husband was the reason for this commotion, this emergency. He's dying, thought Mary Lynn, he's dead. This is not what I wanted, she thought, this is not why I cheated on him, this is not what was supposed to happen.

As more drivers left their cars and ran ahead, Mary Lynn dialed 911 on the cell phone and received only a busy signal.

She opened her door and stepped out, placed one foot on the pavement, and stopped.

The jumper did not stop. She turned to look at the crowd watching her. She looked into the anonymous faces, into the maw, and then looked back down at the black water.

Then she jumped.

Jeremiah rushed forward, along with a few others, and peered over the edge of the bridge. One brave man leapt off the bridge in a vain rescue attempt. Jeremiah stopped a redheaded young man from jumping.

"No," said Jeremiah. "It's too cold. You'll die too."

Jeremiah stared down into the black water, looking for the woman who'd jumped and the man who'd jumped after her.

In the car, or rather with one foot still in the car and one foot placed on the pavement outside of the car, Mary Lynn wept. Oh, God, she loved him, sometimes because he was white and often despite his whiteness. In her fear, she found the one truth Sitting Bull never knew: there was at least one white man who could be trusted.

The black water was silent.

Jeremiah stared down into that silence.

"Jesus, Jesus," said a lovely woman next to him. "Who was she? Who was she?"

"I'm never leaving," Jeremiah said.

"What?" asked the lovely woman, quite confused.

"My wife," said Jeremiah, strangely joyous. "I'm never leaving her." Ever the scientist and mathematician, Jeremiah knew that his wife was a constant. In his relief, he found the one truth Shakespeare never knew: gravity is overrated.

Jeremiah looked up through the crossbeams above him, as he stared at the black sky, at the clouds that he could not see but knew were there, the invisible clouds that covered the stars. He shouted out his wife's name, shouted it so loud that he could not speak in the morning.

In the car, Mary Lynn pounded the steering wheel. With one foot in the car and one foot out, she honked and honked the horn. She wondered if this was how the world was supposed to end, with everybody trapped on a bridge, with the black water pushing against their foundations.

Out on the bridge, four paramedics arrived far too late. Out of breath, exhausted from running across the bridge with medical gear and stretchers, the paramedics could only join the onlookers at the railing.

A boat, a small boat, a miracle, floated through the black water. They found the man, the would-be rescuer, who had jumped into the water after the young woman, but they could not find her.

Jeremiah pushed through the crowd, as he ran away from the place where the woman had jumped. Jeremiah ran across the bridge until he could see Mary Lynn. She and he loved each other across the distance.

# Nelson's Run

PETER BACHO

## prologue 1: a reflection

Lecture: "The Legend of the White Dona of Samar"
Presenter: Dr. Jose Bulaklak, Senior Faculty, University of the Philippines; Distinguished Visiting Professor, University of California at Berkeley
Occasion: Southeast Asian Studies Conference of Washington, Seattle, Washington, 2020

"The legend of the White Dona of Samar, like all such legends, must be placed within the twin contexts of Philippine culture and history. As you know, there are no photographs of the Dona—or 'Bambi,' as some of her followers have reverently called her (apparently a reference to her reputed fawnlike innocence and virginity)—there are just the myriad popular stories and beliefs, which are based on the handful of accounts from those who actually knew her.

"Regarding a cultural and historical context, keep in mind that before the Spaniards came to the Philippines, women played a crucial role in village life. They were the shamans, intermediaries between the village and omnipresent spirit world. That, of course, collided with the arrival of Spain and its especially masculine form of Catholicism. During the course of colonization, the shamans were warned, then punished, then stripped of their powers. The Philippines became Catholic—a religion still fervently practiced today in 2020, or roughly twenty years after the Dona's reported demise.

"But how, you may ask, can an icon so obviously female (note the popular depictions of her full pouty lips, Anglo facial features, and large, fully developed breasts upon which the faithful often place votive candles) so thoroughly grasp the Filipino imagination in a culture that is (on the surface) so male-centered and obviously nonwhite? How indeed.

"And the recent evidence indicates that if anything, her influence grows in all corners of society, ranging from the sacred (the Dona for Sainthood Movement) to the secular (Dona action figures, a Dona for President campaign, and a spate of low-budget Dona movies starring Tori Spelling).

"First, there is the Dona's obvious advantage: she is white, and in a culture which celebrates the colonial past and continues to embrace its values, light skin color is highly prized. Many Filipinos, rightly or wrongly, believe that Caucasian blood 'betters the race.' Note the recent reports from the Island of Leyte, where impoverished citizens have scrimped together enough to purchase a solid gold statue of Donny Osmond; the governor stated the natives would have purchased the entire family, but the cost—given the spiraling numbers of offspring—proved prohibitive. In size, the Donny replica is even greater than that of General Douglas MacArthur, the Philippines' first (some would still argue, greatest) Caucasian icon.

"Note also that figures from the last census (2010) give telling information on Filipino attitudes. There are almost forty million Filipinos in America, or roughly half of the entire Filipino population; most are recent immigrants, or the American-born children of recent immigrants. Surveys indicate they are faithful consumers of peroxides and skin lighteners; the wealthier ones use plastic surgeons (as per the late Michael Jackson, whose pronounced cheekbones and pixie nose tragically collapsed during a recent 'oldies' concert). In fact, at a recent AMA convention, a session was devoted to the development of successful ad campaigns in Tagalog, the national language. The most effective approach was to sell the entire head-to-toe package to prevent what advertisers termed the 'brontosaurus effect,' i.e., a newly narrowed, wrinkle-free, handsomely Anglicized face atop a thin, long neck connected to a still-bulky, still-square body. Once they have acquired U.S. citizenship, these new immigrants almost uniformly vote Republican; they almost always vote for measures directed at nonwhites (note the overwhelming Filipino support for the recent California proposal to shoot on sight illegal Mexican immigrants). Most of the adults came to this country to become Americans, or more specifically, white Americans.

"So, for America's former colonial wards, the lessons of that colonial past have been unusually well absorbed. That absorption has created millions of consumers of American products and the best, most loyal Americans outside of South Carolina's Southern Baptists. This leads to the second point, the seemingly curious rise of a female icon within a male-dominated culture.

"As noted, pre-Hispanic culture revered women. And although Catholicism was established, it is naïve to believe that all traces of previous beliefs simply disappeared. They resurfaced, but in an acceptable manner. For the Catholic Philippines, a woman could exercise enormous political power, but only if she adopted a certain guise. In Catholicism, there is no role more acceptable—or more potent—than that of Mary, Mother of God. Thus, the transgender and cross-dressing beauty pageants that follow religious celebrations—festivities that have been actively promoted by the Bureau of Tourism—often have a religious theme. A typical ad from the island of Cebu featured a poster of the contestants in full female costume and asked residents to vote for the prettiest martyr.

"Thus, in the much-studied 1992 Philippine election, when the Dona reportedly blessed the presidential campaign of Bing Bong Big, the son of the murdered former president, the blessing was widely viewed as a key to his victory. The Dona's influence could not be denied. The roots of that influence stem from the claim of her followers that she was not just Mary incarnate, but from a claim even more astounding, i.e., that she was the mother of the Mother of God.

"As you know, Bing Bong's publicists proclaimed the endorsement and moved quickly to squelch rumors of a sexual quid pro quo for the Dona's support. This was immediately dubbed by the Manila press, noted for its lascivious bent, as 'The Blown Job Scandal.' One of the more famous arguments was that the oral sex she reportedly performed (according to one account from a high administration source who requested anonymity, the Dona 'played the flute,' so to speak); this act, the theory goes, did not rob a virgin of virginity since her own organs remained covered and untouched. Evidently, the electorate agreed, and at one campaign stop, Bing Bong reportedly challenged the 50,000 plus crowd with the following question: 'Who amongst you has not been blown?' Not a hand went up. He then unzipped himself and motioned for one of his aides, reportedly, his choice for Secretary of Defense, to perform fellatio, at which point, he invited the crowd to follow suit. For the next ten minutes, 25,000 of the assembled licked, fondled, and sucked, and the sound, according to one reporter, reminded him the Dona remained a virgin, and thus blessed, and retained her extraordinary level of public adulation and influence.

"Now, I realize that for most of you in the audience, this description may be hard to follow, difficult to accept. However, let me summarize by saying that whatever may be the peculiar cultural beliefs, there are concrete reasons for their existence. . . ."

Overheard at the reception for Dr. Bulaklak: "I love America, just love it. I'm single, you know, eligible to marry. U.S. citizen, of course . . ."

## prologue 2: an overworked axiom—a tree and its falling fruit

The snapshot told it all, or at least enough to catch the curious eye of a three-year-old boy who found it during a brief, unsupervised moment. In that moment, he rummaged freely in a bottom dresser drawer. His mother, unaware, walked into the room to find him staring at his tattered Polaroid treasure, examining a man's pale skin and short blond hair, his liquid blue eyes. To the boy, the image looked familiar.

"Mommy, who?"

"Nelson," she said, trying hard to sound cross. "Naughty, naughty boy. You know you shouldn't be here, and look at this mess. . . ." For effect, she rested her hands on her hips and loudly tapped her toe, language enough, she figured, to abate unwanted three-year-old activity.

This time, though, he ignored her and just kept staring. "Mommy," he replied calmly. "Who?"

When she entered the room, the open drawer, the clothing scattered about—these caught her mother's eye. She didn't see what mattered, what her son was holding, at least not at first.

"Who?"

She inched closer to glance at the photo, then bit her lip. She pulled back and turned away, as if reeling from an invisible punch. If her son had only looked up, he'd have seen her odd reaction, which might have even frightened him. He didn't; he just kept staring.

Breathe deeply, she told herself, again. Again. She turned to face her son, this time with arms open. "Baby," she said. "Come here."

She wiggled her long, tapered fingers for him to come closer, a sign to exchange secrets or share a giggle.

Distracted now, he looked up and turned to the voice. He smiled and took a tiny three-year-old shuffling half step toward her, then returned his gaze to the photo. "Who?" he said.

"Shsss," she scolded, as she gently nuzzled his cheek.

He giggled and squirmed. "Mommy," he protested.

She hugged him and sighed. "Your father," she whispered.

Nelson was daddy's boy, the eldest and only, a junior, in fact, the latest in a very long line. Never mind that his square-jawed, former-track-star daddy preferred to love his son part-time and from afar, and that in lieu of love, Daddy sent cash—lots of it. Young Nelson didn't mind.

Life at home was pleasant; that was all that mattered. Plus, he had company—Mommy, Jerry (his harmless, boring stepdad), and a growing gaggle of half siblings, none of whom resembled Nelson in the least. They were all nice enough, and he was nice back. Jerry and his mother made niceness a religion. Smile and get along, nod and agree, the secrets to life; Nelson learned them early.

About the only disruption in this pleasant predictable routine occurred every July, starting when Nelson was seven. His mother packed him on a jet and flew him west to visit his father. He'd spend at least that month and part of August perched in Daddy's Nob Hill penthouse. During the days, as his father worked to invest, merge, buy or sell, his companion would be a pretty woman much younger than Daddy. For young Nelson, the only problem was that the companions changed every year. One July, when Nelson was ten, Daddy pulled him aside.

"Just call her 'Mom,'" he said, referring to his latest bedmate, a tall redhead with lower-back-length hair who was always wearing sunglasses.

Nelson nodded and smiled. "Sure," he said.

So Mom it was—easy enough, no real name, no memory, no tears on separation. It was that way through the next six Julys, as Daddy's taste ran an ever longer gamut of hair shades and styles—from earthy to elegant—weights (within reason) and heights.

This annual changing of the Moms puzzled Nelson. He didn't particularly miss any of them and, if pressed, couldn't even recall their real names. It's just that Daddy's custom seemed curious, so one July—his thirteenth—when his father and he were alone in the penthouse, he asked why.

"What was wrong with the brunette?" he said, referring to last year's Mom.

"She fell in love, got dependent," he explained. "I got bored." He spoke without emotion or hint of regret, all the while looking at Nelson. "That's just the way they are . . ."

"Women?"

"Yeah, like your mom . . ."

"Which mom?"

Daddy cleared his throat. "The one back in Baltimore," he said. "She was smart, driven, but then, after a while, she just got that way, they all do." He paused. "So I left, but that, ah, that doesn't mean I didn't want you or, ah, don't care. Hell, you're my boy, my blood, and besides, you're here, aren't you? It just means, well, you know . . ."

"Uh-huh."

Nelson followed Daddy's blue eyes; their gaze seemed to float to the ceiling, lingering awhile before shifting to the far wall, only to fall, then rise again to focus on him. Nelson stared back.

"Yeah, and when it gets like that," Daddy began, "it's just best to keep going, to start running." He paused. "We're men, and I'm including you, son," he said solemnly. "We're white men, we're rich, we make the rules. Oh, I know it's not popular nowadays, so you have to be careful, but truth is truth. We're not all equal. It's no one's fault, it's just the way it is."

Young Nelson nodded.

"Ever hear of Darwin?"

"Who?"

"Charles Darwin."

"Uh-uh."

"Never mind," Daddy continued. "All you need to know is that nature's logical; it's got a ladder, and white men are on the top rung. Well, at least some of us. That's our niche, we run things—companies, governments, hell, even television. That's natural. Ayn Rand just kinda updates Darwin, at least in my view. In case you haven't noticed, this damn town's crawling with Chinamen, but you'll never see one on TV, unless he's Hop Sing, but that's OK because that's just natural."

"Ayn who?"

"You know, the writer . . . 'The word which can never die . . . The sacred word: EGO,'" Daddy whispered, eyes closed, as if on his knees in prayer.

"Huh?"

"She wrote that."

"Who?"

"Ayn Rand. I've got all her works in the library, hard cover first edition, of course. You should read them."

"But she's a woman . . ."

"So what, she's ugly as sin," Daddy said. "Looks like a man, writes like one, too." He paused. "She's one of us, except for the ugly part, of course."

"OK, I guess . . ."

"And that's the problem with women, except old Ayn; they're not where we are, they reject their niche. Worse, they resent yours, so they'll try to drag you down. Son, you just can't let that happen, can't let 'em do that. Let them go before they get that way, it's a cost-benefit deal."

"Cost-benefit?"

"Yeah, cost-benefit. It just means that sometimes it stops being worth it, like keeping the same woman, that's all," he said, and looked at Nelson to see if he understood. Daddy still wasn't sure. Probably too young, he guessed, but he'd done his duty, explained himself, explained science, covered his tracks to his son's Daddyless past. He'd conveyed, as best he could, these most important truths as he knew them. He rubbed his palms together before looking at his watch—a business dinner tonight, thank God— then glanced at his son, who was smiling and nodding. He smiled and nodded back.

Daddy cleared his throat. "Women, you know what I mean," he said with a wink. Maybe he didn't, but Nelson being his son, he knew he'd figure it out soon enough.

"Gotta get ready," Daddy said, and put his hand on Nelson's shoulder. As he turned and walked away, Nelson studied him. He was tall, long limbed, still athletic—pretty good for a middle-aged white guy.

"Your mom says you're a runner," he heard Daddy say from his bedroom.

"Pardon?"

"A track man."

"Oh."

"Are you fast?"

"I suppose."

Nelson heard him laugh. "You can thank me for that."

"Pardon?"

"Genetics, son. You're either born a runner or you're not. It's a great talent, believe me, the best." Nelson heard him laugh again. "The best."

Over the next two summers, as Nelson bloomed, the resemblance to Daddy became even more striking, like his mom had contributed nothing to him other than a warm human wetland to gestate. He was tall, taller than his namesake, and rawboned, all angles, long arms and legs. In San Francisco during his sixteenth summer, the point was made by the latest Mom, an especially stunning one, who kept mentioning to Nelson the eerily close father/son resemblance.

This Mom was different, right from the start, Daddy and her together, Gate 22, incoming from Baltimore. Daddy strode forward to greet him; Mom stood behind. During his Baltimore months, Nelson had taken to wearing shades, all his tony, too-cool pals did, but even through the tint, as his eyes darted between the two, he could tell: this Mom was different.

For one, she was younger than the others—early twenties, maybe even less. For another, she wasn't white; not black, but definitely colored.

A firm handshake, a meeting of an original and its latest and only variation. Daddy smiled and gave a casual, wordless shrug in her direction. She stood back, silent. Nelson dipped his head and peered over his glasses. Brown, he thought, she was brown with shiny black hair cut in a stylish bob, the ends of which touched the nape of a long, thin neck. Black and white he understood, or assumed he did. Back in Baltimore, there were plenty of both. But brown? Odd. An island girl maybe, but which island, atoll, or archipelago. Just where had Daddy found her?

Another Daddy sign—a second subtle shrug—and they started to move, inching themselves away from the mob at the gate and toward the terminal lobby.

"Pit stop," Daddy airily announced with a wave of his hand. This newest, oddest Mom slowed and stopped, still silent as wall paint, as Daddy and he disappeared into the men's room.

"You're probably wondering," Daddy began as they hovered over adjoining urinals.

"Well . . ."

"My choice," he explained. "I'm entitled to variety, a different taste, and when you're us, you got choices." He smiled. "My first colored girl," he whispered, then turned to scan the room. Except for them, it was empty. "Sweet," he said loudly as he rolled his eyes. "And she just loves it, believe me, a little brown sex machine."

"But I thought you said . . ."

Daddy shrugged. "Jefferson did it."

"Jefferson?"

"Jefferson, you know, the second president." He paused and shook himself, coaxing free a few more drops. "Or maybe the third . . ."

"Did what?"

"Screwed colored girls."

"But she's not Negro."

"You're right, she's better," he explained. "An island gook straight out of *South Pacific*, the movie, I mean. Ever see it? She's exotic, passive, presentable. A perfect quiet fit on any white man's arm. My kind of colored.

"That old boy knew what he was doing," he said as he reached for his zipper. "He lived by his own rules, founded a damn country, too."

Nelson glanced at Daddy, still above the urinal, hand still on his zipper. He'd closed his eyes; the corners of his mouth twitched upward to form a faint smile. "History," Daddy said softly, as if in prayer. "Gotta know it, at least the part that's useful."

Nelson smiled too and added just the slightest of nods.

That summer, Daddy was busier than usual. A week before Nelson had arrived, his father had brokered a multidepartment store merger that began well enough—blue-suited smiles and handshakes, backslaps, lit cigars, the usual signs of wealthy old white guy bonhomie. Then, as Daddy told it, the majority stock–holding grandson of the founder of one of the stores—the smallest one—suddenly crapped on the deal. He objected, claiming he'd seen gramps in a dream. The old man was wearing rags (mismatched pieces off the bargain rack) and selling pencils. Grandson took it as an omen to stop the merger.

The news reached Daddy the morning after Nelson arrived. The rest of that day, Daddy was a dervish. He called the grandson at his home in Boston, trying to persuade him to change his mind. Failing that, he made other calls and was constantly rushing in and out of the condominium. That evening, the three of them—Daddy, Mom, and Nelson—drove to the airport and, along the way, stopped briefly on Dolores Street to add a fourth—an old Gypsy-looking woman, complete with dark, angled features, crystal ball, and bandana.

"Daddy," Nelson began. "When are you and your associate, ah . . ."

"Lazonga," she said, unsmiling. Lazonga handed him a card, which Nelson glanced at. "Prognosticator," the card read. "Cash only, no checks."

"Right," Nelson mumbled.

Daddy chuckled as the car pulled quickly into an unloading zone. He hopped out, followed by his new "associate," then leaned over and motioned for Nelson to roll down his window.

"When are you coming home?" Nelson asked.

Daddy chuckled. "When the dickhead gets a new dream."

The return trip to Nob Hill was, for Nelson, a list of firsts. He noticed for the first time that the Bay, just west of the freeway, glistened at night, and that unlike during the day, there was no breeze or bluster, not even a whisper. Another first. As was his first close inspection of Mom, who was driving and wearing a very short linen dress, the hem of which seemed by the minute to be inching north. When she floored the accelerator—quite often, he thought—the muscles of her brown and bare right thigh, calf, ankle, and toes flexed and flowed not unlike a dancer's sensual extension. To not seem rude (or lascivious), he tried not to stare; he'd look straight ahead, or at the Bay, but would always manage to roll his eyes to his left and down, or turn just so to see if the hem was continuing its northward trek.

It was. This time the stop was crotch level where her panties should have been but weren't. Nelson blinked and looked again. None. He gulped. A woman without underwear was dangerous, at least according to Robert, a neighborhood friend, who swore he'd done a pantyless public school girl and survived, but just barely.

He gulped again when he noticed that noticing this movement of fabric had made him bulge. He hoped she didn't notice. It was so improper, untoward.

Some of his Baltimore prep school pals had had sex, a daring move in the 1970s, but it was always with private school girls, brimming with good blood, fat trust accounts, loosely guarded virginity—and only after false claims of love and pro forma attempts to resist. Like this last spring prom (backseat and braless/finger then tongue), but then she blurted "love" and the moment, at least for Nelson, vanished.

To the best of his knowledge, not one of his peers had ever done his father's lover, and that included the adventurous Robert. Plus, this one was some kind of colored—they're different, all prep school white boys knew, just watch them dance—and the closest any of his group had gotten to one of those was the daughter of the Spanish ambassador. Still, old Jefferson had found something; he'd heard the drums, felt the rhythm, tasted the sweat. He'd crossed a racial line, spent his nights there, and still founded a country. Late in life, Daddy found him worthy of emulation; early in his, Nelson hoped he would, too.

Nelson wondered how he'd approach her. She was older, obviously experienced, undoubtedly dangerous; she wasn't his prom date. Just thinking about it made him stretch even more, then twitch. His hands dampened. To cover his reaction, he began to chatter nervously. "So," he mumbled. "What's your name?"

"Mom," she said, as she gunned the gas pedal. Centrifugal force threw Nelson back, but not hard enough that he couldn't sneak a peek at his newly favorite sight. Sweet, he thought.

"You know, I mean, uh, your real name." Nelson silently cursed. Lame, he thought.

She turned slightly and smiled, then took his hand and placed it on her upper thigh. "Start here and work up," she whispered. "Then maybe I'll tell you."

That night in Daddy's spacious bedroom would be another Nelson first. He paused at the doorway, thinking he should be feeling something—a jolt of conscience, a whisper of guilt. But none, not a shadow or hint. As he lingered, Mom had passed, gone right in; he watched as she slowly undressed, graceful as a cat, starting with the skirt which slid to her ankles. Daintily, she stepped out and kicked it to a corner. Nelson could see the smile, hear her purr (or he thought she did); vision and sound pulled him forward.

"Come," she said. "Don't be afraid."

"I'm not," he lied.

As he, heart pounding, neared the bed, his brief reverie returned to hector him. It should somehow be harder, he thought, to betray his own flesh, but it wasn't. He unzipped his pants. She smiled again, and before it faded, he was beside her on the bed.

She snuggled next to him; awkwardly, he enfolded her, and could feel her fingernails gently raking his back, her toes dragging up and down his shins, then stopping. Her toes probed, curled, and pulled. She giggled. "Socks, Nelson." She paused. "You're wearing socks, crew socks at that. Is that how it's done in Baltimore?"

"Yes," he mumbled.

"Ah, America," she sighed. "So blond, so strange."

"What?"

"I bet they're striped."

"So what?" he said defensively.

Nelson soon lost his socks, then his virginity, as Mom—her body taut, her loving flexible, athletic—twisted and bent him, always coaxing one last squirt. She moaned and bit him, he bucked and bit back. It was dawn when they untangled, unwrapping themselves from each other and the sweat-stained, hair-matted sheets.

"Damn," Nelson whispered, as he rolled on his back. "What's your name?"

"Sylvia," she replied. "But you can still call me Mom."

So Sylvia stayed Mom from that early morning on, even through later nights, afternoons, and twilights—or when Daddy was gone (often), or not paying attention (also often). During one session, she told him bits of herself—that she was twenty, born in Manila, hiding in America, down to her last buck and nursing a beer at an upscale Embarcadero bar, when Daddy sidled up and bought her another. That led to more rounds and a smooth black leather billfold that opened slowly to flash a multicolored plastic collage against a solid backdrop of green. She and Daddy told stories that night. Hers: her visa had expired, but she didn't want to return. His: he loved Orientals (including, on this night, Hop Sing). Of course, Daddy didn't, but he sensed a kill. His smile summoned the manager, whom he greeted with a nickname; he signed for the check.

"An economic move." She sighed and gazed at her lover. "He's pink, you know, and small enough to hold in my palm, even when he's hard. Close and it's gone. Worse, he's so predictable, no imagination. Him on top—enter, wiggle twice, squirt, groan, pull out. For all he'd notice, I could be doing my nails. I fake it, he's happy, I stay in America." She smiled at Nelson. "But you're not like that, not at all. You're darker, larger . . ."

The comparison made him nervous. "Mom . . ."

" . . . much more imaginative."

Nelson shook his head.

"I know, he's your father," she said. "But truth is truth, there's no comparison. You're better, the latest and best model—an evolving, adapting species. Darwin would be proud."

"Darwin?"

"Your father's always talking about him." She giggled mischievously. "I can't wait for your son."


The end came without any drama or even much stress—Daddy never found out—just vacation's end and the parting of ways. As the time for departure drew nearer, Nelson and Mom, as if by silent mutual accord, began pulling back, so much so that she didn't even go with him to the airport. He went by cab; Daddy was again out of town, an absence that relieved Nelson—no feigned affection necessary. At the boarding gate, just for the briefest moment, Nelson wondered about it—what had passed and his odd detachment—but by midpoint, somewhere over Nebraska, even Mom was a ghost of a summer now gone. No sense to mope or dwell. It was time, he figured, to start planning ahead.

Back in Baltimore, Nelson plunged into the school year, loping through classes on personality and acceptable attendance; he also dabbled at track, showing just enough talent to torment his coaches, who'd urge him to push. Why? he'd ask, he was winning. But always on dabble and talent, they'd answer, never on heart. Besides, his focus was elsewhere, on women, not prep school girls, and spare moments—which seemed to increase—were given to their pursuit, mostly at local colleges, where his height, broad shoulders, and the premature appearance of facial hair allowed him to blend in. Each weekend, and some weekday nights, he was more successful than not—his apprenticeship with Mom had served him well.

Nelson never pined for Mom—he was much too busy—although she seemed to pine for him via the occasional letter, the whispered late-night call. What could he say? That he missed her? Maybe next summer, he'd say, we'll see—tepid enough replies to slow down, then finally stop, both letter and whispered call, until one spring afternoon, near the start of Easter Break, Mom called again. She was crying.

"He's dead, Nelson," she began.

"Who?"

"Your father."

Nelson gasped. "How?"

"I killed him," she said between sobs. "Didn't mean to, but I guess I did."

"Uh, Mom . . ."

"One night, I was doing my nails right there on the bed," she began. "And your father came home late from out of town. He was tipsy and he wanted to have sex, so I lay on my back, and he mounts me and . . ."

"And what?"

"I kept doing my nails." She paused. "He'd never noticed before, but this time he did and boy, was he mad. He slapped me and told me to get out, that he'd call Immigration, have me deported. I slapped him back. He tried to choke me. I stabbed him in the eardrum."

"With what?"

"My nail file." She was sobbing now.

"Mom."

"It was an accident," she howled. "I was aiming for an eye, a flesh wound."

"Flesh wound?"

"But then he turned and started bleeding, getting still and cold," she said. "And I guess I also must have blown up, ah, certain parts of him with firecrackers, big ones, rockets, that sort of thing, leftovers from Chinese New Year. At least that's what the police said after they stopped fainting. Myself, I don't recall."

"Damn."

"Nelson, I'm desperate," she wailed. "I need cash, the best attorney. I need you. You're rich now, his sole beneficiary. If I get out of this, we can be together."

"Mom, we'll see," Nelson said flatly, and hung up the phone. He took a deep breath. His father was dead, his old lover was in jail, and he was suddenly very rich. He'd send her a check, help her out. He didn't think he'd visit, though—the costs of reinvolvement clearly outweighed the benefits. Nelson glanced at his watch and smiled. Besides, he had a date with Diana, a studious comp-lit major with long hair and firm breasts. She lived across town; he still needed to shower. She wore glasses; he wondered how she'd look without them.

# Godoy Lives

DANIEL CHACÓN

Juan's cousin wrote what he knew of the dead guy. He was from Jalisco. Not married. Some called him *maricón* because they suspected he was gay, but no one knew for sure.

The age of the man was the same as Juan's, twenty-four, and the picture on the green card strikingly similar, sunken cheeks, small forehead, tiny, deep-set eyes that on Juan looked as if everything scared him, but that on the dead guy looked focused, confident. "You could use this to come work here," his cousin wrote.

It was perfect, Juan thought, if not for the name written on the green card: Miguel Valencia Godoy.

Godoy? Juan wasn't even sure how to pronounce it. His wife Maria held the green card in her small, work-gnarled hand and she looked at the name, then at Juan.

"Goo doy," she said.

He tried: "Guld Yoy."

Patiently she took a breath. "Goo doy."

He practiced and practiced. It got so the entire family was saying it: Maria, their four-year-old boy, Juan Jr., and even the big-eyed baby girl came close with "goo goo." Only Juan couldn't say it. Some nights Maria kept him up late, pushing him awake as he dozed off, until he said it correctly three times in a row.

When the day came for him to leave, he kissed her good-bye, shook his son's hand like a man, and kissed the baby's soft, warm head. The treeless dirt road stretched into the barren hills, reaching the nearest town seven miles away where he would catch the bus to Tijuana.

"I'll be back," he said to Maria.

"I know you will," she said.

"I'll send money when I find work."

"I know you will," she said. She placed a palm on his face. "You're a good man, Juan. I know you'll do what's right."

He looked into her eyes, disappointed that he could not find in them a single tear. She smiled sadly, like a mother sending her child off to school.

"Go, Juan," she said. "Don't make this harder than it needs to be."

"I can't help it," he wept. She hugged him in her strong, bony arms. She smelled of body odor. "Don't do this. Be a man," she said firmly.

He pulled away from her, wiped his tears, and said, "I'm going."

"Again," she said.

"Duld Woy," he sniveled.

"Goo doy. Again."

"Goose boy."

"Juan, if you don't get it, things will be bad."

At the border, he nervously stepped across a red line painted on the sidewalk. He stepped past warning signs that ordered people to turn back if not able to enter the U.S. Inside the building, big and bright as an indoor sports stadium, he was surprised at the number of Mexicans waiting in line to get to the U.S. side. Still, most of the people were white, holding bags of souvenirs, colorful Mexican blankets, ceramics, bottles of tequila. He looked at the heads of the lines to see which U.S. immigration officer he should approach.

People who knew had told him that the worst immigration officers in the U.S. were the ones of Mexican descent. Pick a white officer, he had heard, because the Mexican American—the Chicano—INS officers had to prove to the white people that they were no longer Mexicans. He had heard that they would beat people up in the mountains or sic vicious dogs on them, laughing as the bloody flesh flew in all directions.

There were three open lines, three officers, a white woman, and two white men. He chose a young man with a shaved head whose line moved fast because he barely looked at the IDs held out to him, just waved everyone through, bored, like he didn't want to be there.

Juan knew that this would be easier than he had imagined. With a confidence he had never felt before, he said to himself, slightly out loud, in perfect pronunciation, "Godoy."

When he was two people from the front, something terrible happened. A tall Chicano officer tapped the white agent on the shoulder and said something. The white guy smiled, stood up, and left, leaving the tall Chicano to take his place. This Mexican American was mean looking, well over six feet tall, with massive shoulders and legs thick as tree trunks. His green INS uniform stretched like a football player's. Set below his flat forehead, above his chubby cheeks, were small black eyes that darted suspiciously from face to face. His hair was cut short to his head, sticking straight up, and he didn't smile.

Juan wanted to get out of the line, but he was next.

The Chicano looked down at him. "Why should I let you through?" he demanded in English.

Juan didn't understand a word except for "you" which he believed meant him, but he assumed the officer had asked for his green card, so he held it up.

And smiled.

The Chicano looked suspiciously into Juan's eyes. He grabbed the card from his fingers and looked closely at the picture, then back at Juan.

"What's your name?" he asked in Spanish.

Juan took a deep breath and said, "Miguel Valencia Goo poo."

"*What?*" asked the officer, chest inflating with air.

Juan was sure he'd be grabbed by the collar and dragged out.

He tried again: "Miguel Valencia Godoy."

"What's that last name?"

Sweat trickled down his back.

"Godoy?" he offered.

"Where are you from?"

"Jalisco," he remembered.

The officer put the ID card on the counter and said, with a big smile, "Cousin! It's me!"

He had said it in Spanish, but to Juan the words still had no meaning.

"I'm your cousin. Francisco Pancho Montes Godoy."

"Oh?"

"Don't you remember me?"

"Oh, Pancho, of course," said Juan, weakly.

"You lying son of a bitch," said Pancho. "You don't even recognize me. Come on," he said, coming around the counter. "I know what to do with guys like you." He picked up the duffel bag as effortlessly as if it were a purse, and led Juan across the vast floor of the building, through crowds of people, into a little room with chairs, a TV, and magazines in English. Pancho dropped the bag, turned around, and said, *"Un abrazo,"* holding out his long and thick arms. He hugged the breath out of Juan. He smelled of freshly cleaned laundry. Then he held him at arm's length to get a better look. "You haven't changed. You wait right here. When I get off, I'm taking you home. You can see my wife and kids." He started to walk out, but something struck him. He turned around. "Oh, I just thought of something."

"What?"

"Really. It just occurred to me."

"What did?"

"I have a special surprise for you, Miguel."

"What surprise?" asked Juan.

"You'll see," said Pancho. "A surprise."

Juan waited about three hours in that room. One time he tried to escape, but when he opened the door, Pancho, from behind the counter, looked right at him and winked.

At last, Pancho opened the door. He was now dressed in street clothes, 501 jeans and a T-shirt with a faded image of Mickey Mouse. He looked like a giant kid.

"Come on, cousin," he said. "I'm taking you home."

Like a lamb led to the slaughter, Juan followed through the parking lot, looking between the rows for an escape route, Pancho's shadow stretching across the hoods of several cars. Pancho grabbed him by the arm with a strong grip and escorted him to the passenger side of an oversized Ford pickup. Juan pictured Maria wearing a black dress and veil, standing over his grave, not weeping, just shaking her head, saying, "Dumb, Juan. Why can't he do nothing right?"

He climbed up into the cab, using both hands and feet, like a child climbing a tree. He had to get out of there quick, find his real cousin, the one who had sent him the dead man's green card, and work his ass off so he could send Maria money. She needed him. His family needed him.

They drove through town, the truck so high off the ground Juan thought that surely this must be what it was like to be on a horse. He held on to the rim of the seat.

"Hey, cousin. Listen to me," Pancho said. "You'll never guess the surprise I have for you."

"What is it?" Juan asked.

Pancho laughed an evil laugh, an "I got you now" laugh.

"You'll see," he said.

"Can you give me a hint?"

"You won't be disappointed. So, tell me, where have you been these last years?"

"I'm not married," Juan said, remembering another detail about Godoy.

"Oh?" Pancho asked.

"Never found someone I loved," he said.

"Well, here you'll find plenty of women. Lorena has a pretty sister. Lorena turned out to be the greatest wife in the world."

Juan wanted to say no, that Maria was the greatest, but he couldn't.

He had seen her at an outdoor dance in the *zócalo* of a nearby town one sunny Sunday afternoon. She was the prettiest girl there, wearing a white dress that fell just above her knees, her cinnamon-colored legs smooth and shapely. She was seventeen. All afternoon guys stood around her like giants, boys with large shoulders, black cowboy boots, and white straw cowboy hats that shined in the sun, while Juan, a skinny, sickly-looking boy barely eighteen, watched her from behind the balloon vendor. Still, Maria noticed him.

As was the custom, the unmarried young people walked in a circle at the center of the plaza, girls in one direction, boys in another, and although several girls were available, most of the boys eyed Maria, and when they passed her, they threw confetti in her long black hair or they offered their hands to her, but she walked by each of them, looking at Juan the entire time. He in turn looked over his shoulder at the tiled dome of the cathedral, convinced she was looking past him. Since she was rejecting so many others, he decided it wouldn't be so bad when she rejected him, so he was determined to throw some confetti in her hair. When she was right beside him, he raised his clenched hand, but when he opened it, he realized he had nothing. *What a fool I am!* he cried to himself. But Maria brushed out the confetti already in her hair and offered him her hand. So excited, he wasn't sure with which hand to take hers, extending one, withdrawing it, extending the other, so she took control. She grabbed his arm and led him away from the circle.

Pancho pulled the truck into a gravel lot lined by a three-foot-tall chain-link fence that surrounded a large front yard and a small house. Two dogs barked at the truck, a German shepherd and a big black Lab. "Here we are, *primo*," he said. "This is home."

Pancho opened the fence and the dogs jumped on him for affection, but then they stopped and seemed to wait for Juan to enter the yard, their tongues hanging out, tails wagging, whining as if unable to contain their excitement.

"Do they bite?" Juan asked.

"Don't worry, they only bite strangers," said Pancho.

"That's good," Juan said. The dogs surrounded him, sniffing his crotch, his legs, the Michoacán dirt caked to his boots.

The men entered the house, which had purple shag carpet and a velveteen couch and love seat. The painting above the TV was a velvet likeness of the Aztec warrior with the dead woman in his arms. The place smelled of beans cooking.

"Lorena," called Pancho. "He's here." Then he looked at Juan. "I called her and told her you'd be coming."

Lorena, a strikingly handsome woman in a jean skirt, which came above her knees, and a white T-shirt that hugged her voluptuous body, walked in, wiping her hands on a dishtowel. Standing next to each other, she and her husband looked like the perfect couple, him tall and broad-shouldered, a little chubby around the middle and on the face, and her, tall, big boned, wide hips. She had a long jaw like an Indian and long black hair tied in a ponytail.

"I don't believe it," she said. She ran up and gave Juan a big hug. Her flesh was soft and pillowy, and she smelled of fresh onions. She held him at arm's length. "This is such a wonderful day. Imagine," she said. "Just imagine."

"Imagine," Pancho said, his hands on his hips, smiling big.

Juan wasn't sure if Godoy had ever met Lorena, so he wasn't sure what to say. He said, "Imagine."

"I have your room ready for you," she said. "Do you want to wash up or rest?"

"Later," said Pancho. "First he has to meet the girls."

He led Juan down the hallway. Framed family pictures lined the walls. At one metal frame with multiple photos, Pancho stopped and pointed to two little kids dressed like cowboys, holding toy guns and trying to look mean. "You remember that?"

It was Pancho and the dead man as kids. Juan looked close. The similarities between that child and how he remembered looking as a child were so great that it spooked him, as if he had had all his life two lives that went on simultaneously. He almost remembered that day playing cowboys.

"That was in Jalisco," Juan said.

"That's right. On grandfather's ranch. Remember that ranch?"

Juan pictured acres of land, a stable with twenty of the finest horses, and a garden where the family ate dinner, served by Indians, on a long wooden table. "Do I," he said dreamily.

"And all those horses," Pancho said, sadly delighted. "Oh, well, come on. We have plenty of time to reminisce, but first I want you to meet the girls."

Juan expected that he was referring to Lorena's sisters, but when Pancho opened a bedroom door, two little girls, five-year-old black-eyed twins, sat on the floor playing with dolls. They looked up at their father. "Hello, Daddy," they said in unison.

"Come here, sweethearts. I want you to meet someone."

Obediently they rose and came to their father, standing on either side of him. "This is your *Tío* Miguel."

Both girls ran to Juan and hugged him. "Hi, *tío*. We love you."

They smelled of baby powder.

Lorena insisted he go to bed early because of his long journey, so after dinner—chile verde with fat flour tortillas—she led him into the extra bedroom and clicked on a table lamp, an arc of light appearing like a holy apparition across the white wall. Their shadows were so tall that their heads touched the ceiling. She showed him the shower and where they kept the towels. When she bent over to explain how to use the stereo, her T-shirt hung open, exposing her cleavage. She slowly kissed him on the forehead, soft, wet lips, and she left him alone. As he lay in bed he felt himself aroused. As much as he tried to picture Maria, he couldn't stop seeing Lorena, nor could he help but fantasize what her sister looked like. He reached in his underwear and felt for himself, but on the high part of the wall, above the shadow of his horizontal body, in the arc of light, he saw an image of Maria wearing a veil, shaking her head. He turned off the lamp.

The next day Pancho woke him early and said it was his day off and he'd show Juan around.

"And tomorrow I'm calling in sick. We have so much to do."

As they drove through the city, Juan said, "I need to work, *primo*. I need a job."

"What are you going to do?" said Pancho.

"I have some connections in Fresno," said Juan. "I thought I'd go there and pick fruit."

Pancho laughed. "That's wetback work."

I *am* a wetback, Juan thought. But he said, "I'm not experienced enough at anything else."

"Miguel. Miguelito," said Pancho, shaking his head. His chubby cheeks were slightly pockmarked from acne as a teenager. "I got it all figured out, *primo*. Don't worry."

They drove out of town onto a narrow, two-lane highway lined by tall pine trees, until they reached a clearing, a vast green ranch set in a glen, beyond which the ocean lay over the horizon like a sparkling blue sheet. They entered a white gate with the name of the ranch, *Cielito Lindo*, and drove on the paved driveway until they reached a three-story Spanish-style hacienda.

"What is this place?" Juan asked.

"You'll see."

A white man in his fifties walked out of the mansion. He wore tight jeans and a flannel shirt tucked in and was in good shape for his age. His gray hair was balding on the top. He smiled as he approached Juan, extending his hand. "Welcome, Miguel. My name's BD. Pancho told me all about you and the funny thing that happened at the border." Although he spoke with a U.S. accent, he spoke Spanish well.

"Yes, it was very funny," Juan said.

"What are the chances?" BD said.

BD led them around the mansion to the stables, white wooden buildings with so many doors extending on the horizon that it looked like a mirror image of itself. People led horses in and out of the doors. They entered one and saw horses proudly standing in their stalls, white and black Arabians, their nostrils flaring as if aware of their own worth. A Mexican man was brushing one of them, and as he stroked her silky neck, he cooed how beautiful she was.

"Memo," BD said to the man.

Memo looked up.

"This is Miguel Godoy. He's going to join our team."

"It's very nice to meet you," said Juan.

"Guillermo Reyes," the man said, extending his hand to Juan. "Godoy you say? Is that a Mexican name?"

"Of course it is," said Juan.

"Well, the name itself isn't," said Pancho. "But our family is pure Mexican. Although we're the first generation of American," he said, proudly putting his arm around Juan.

Memo's eyes scrutinized Juan. "Are you from Michoacán?"

"No, hell no. He's from Jalisco," said Pancho, offended by the thought.

"You sound like you're from Michoacán," Memo said.

Over iced tea under a white gazebo, BD explained how he became part owner of the ranch when he was Pancho's age, twenty-five, and he had invested money in the land with four other partners. Over the years they built the country club, the stables, and bought twenty more acres on which their customers rode the horses. Some of the horses they took care of for the rich and famous. BD, who worked as an INS officer with Pancho, would retire in a few years a rich man. "I'll spend all my time out here."

"See, cousin, that's the secret of success. You spend your lifetime investing. Right now I'm thinking about buying into an apartment building. We'll invest our money together, cousin, and we'll be rich."

"What money?" Juan asked.

"What money," Pancho repeated, laughing.

Juan's job at the ranch, BD explained, was to take the horses out of the stable for the customers, make sure they got mounted safely, and then when they return them, turn the horses over to Memo or another stable hand.

"But I don't speak English," Juan said.

"What a great way to learn," Pancho said.

"I don't know anything about horses," Juan said.

"He's being modest," Pancho said. "He has a gift."

When BD told Juan how much he'd be earning, Juan had to hear it again to be certain he had heard right.

"And the best part of it is," said Pancho, "tax free. Cash."

That evening Lorena's sister, Elida, an eighteen-year-old with light brown hair and golden eyes, had dinner with the family. She was so beautiful that Juan couldn't stop sneaking looks at her, and she frequently looked at him and shyly smiled, which made the little black-eyed twins put their tiny hands over their mouths and giggle. When Pancho broke out with the stories about Miguel as a child, how brave he was and how everyone knew he'd be a great man, how girls used to follow him around, about the fights he'd get into with older and bigger boys, Elida looked at him with a stare that bordered on awe. Juan relished the stories, picturing it all and almost believing that he had done those things. After dinner, while the family was drinking coffee and the little girls were munching their dessert, Juan stood up and said he'd like to get some fresh air. He looked at Elida and asked if she would join him.

She said she'd love to.

On the patio they sat on the swing. The full moon shone like a cross in the black sky and reflected in Elida's large eyes. Her face was smooth. The sweet smell of her perfume rose like curls of smoke and swam into his nose, reaching so far into him that they massaged his heart. "Can I touch your face?" he said.

"My face? That's funny. Why for would you want to do that?"

Her Spanish wasn't that good, but she had probably never been to Mexico.

"Because it's the most beautiful face I have ever seen."

She lowered her eyes. He kept looking at the smoothness of her skin, down her thin neck—a birthmark at the protruding bone. At her breasts.

"Okay," she said. "You can touch."

He looked up.

He reached out his hand, opened his palm, and as if he were touching something sacred, he slowly felt the warmth of her face. Passionately, she pressed her cheek into his hand and she closed her eyes and sighed. "That's nice," she said, opening her eyes and looking into his.

Lorena called them inside to watch a movie they had rented. Side by side on the love seat, they glanced as often at each other as they did at the TV. When it was over, Elida said she had to get home. Juan walked her to the car. She opened the door, but before she got in she turned around, bit her bottom lip, and peered at him with eyes that spoke of desire. "I guess I'll see you later," she said.

"You will."

He watched her pull onto the street and her taillights disappear into the darkness.

When he went back into the house, Pancho and Lorena were waiting for him, standing side by side, big smiles on their faces.

Although it hadn't been two days, these two seemed so familiar, so much like family. It occurred to him that he could keep this up for a long time, maybe forever. They would never know. Juan, quite frankly, was having a good time.

What was the rush to work in those hot fields, making less in one month than what he'd make in a week at the stables? He could still send Maria money.

Maria.

She didn't even cry when he left. She was probably glad he was gone.

"Well, cousin, tell us," Pancho said, as if he couldn't stand the anticipation. "What did you think of Lorena's sister?"

Juan laughed, heading toward the hallway to his bedroom, and he said, as if the question carried its own answer, "What did I think of Lorena's sister."

Life was great.

He made plenty of money, much of which he spent taking Elida to restaurants. He was beginning to learn English, and Pancho wanted them to invest in real estate together, as a team. When Juan reminded him he didn't have much money, Pancho assured him it would work out. "I don't think that'll be a problem," he said. One day at work, feeling good after a night with Elida, wherein they went further than they ever had, although not all the way, he was friendly and joked with the customers in English. Around midday, he got this urge to have lunch with someone, to click glasses with an old friend. In the stables he searched for Memo but couldn't find him, not in the country club or walking around the grounds. Finally, as he was walking around the back of the stables, he saw him on a picnic table eating lunch with what must have been his family, his wife and two kids, a little boy and a little girl. They weren't talking as they ate. They just ate, but it was a such a picture of happiness that for the first time in a long time, he thought of his own kids, Juan Jr., the baby, and he felt a great loss for his Maria.

What was she going to do without him? The right thing to do would be to take the money he had already earned, perhaps earn a little more, and send it to Maria. Wherever she was at that moment, whatever she was doing, there was no doubt in her mind that he was going to come back. He had to quit seeing Elida.

Later that night they were walking along the pier in San Diego when he was going to tell her it was over between them. He said, "I think you should know something."

Elida stopped walking and looked at him. Her eyes filled with love and hope. Anticipation.

"I love you," he blurted.

They kissed.

Later that night in her small bedroom plastered with glossy Ricky Martin posters, they made love. Her parents were out of town. Afterward, as he held her smooth body in his thin arms, the smell of her perfume mixing with the scent of the peach-scented candle flickering on her nightstand, he told her that he never wanted to be without her. And he meant it. He was in love.

When he got home, Pancho was sitting on the couch waiting for him, his big legs crossed, his arm extended across the back of the sofa.

"What's up?" Juan asked.

"Remember that surprise I told you about?"

"What surprise?" asked Juan.

"When I first saw you at the border. I told you I had a surprise for you."

"Oh yeah," said Juan.

"Well, tomorrow I'm going to let you have it," he said, standing up.

When Juan woke up the next morning, Pancho had already left. He found Lorena in the kitchen cutting a melon into bite-sized slices. She told him that Pancho went to get the surprise. As she served him a plate of the melon and a cup of strong black coffee, she saw the concern in his face. "Don't worry so much," she said as she sat at the table opposite him.

He remained silent, worried.

"You *do* like it here with me and Pancho, right?"

He was distracted, but he still said yes.

"Look," she said, feeling sorry for him. "I think what Pancho's doing is wrong. I told him so. If you're not prepared for it, things could be difficult."

"What are you talking about?"

"The surprise. I told him not to do it this way, but he wouldn't listen. Sometimes he doesn't think things out fully. This is one of those times."

"What's the surprise?" asked Juan.

"Okay, I'm going to tell you," Lorena said. "But only because I don't think it's right what he's doing."

Pancho went to the Greyhound bus station, she said, to pick up Godoy's mother, who had been living in El Paso. He was bringing her here so she could live with Miguel, her only living son.

The world fell on him. It was over. A mother would always know who her son was. "Don't worry," said Lorena. "She'll be so happy to see you. She never stopped being your mother."

After eating a couple of pieces of melon and drinking coffee, Juan said he wasn't feeling well and wanted to lie down. When he got into his bedroom, he quickly pulled the dirty duffel bag from the closet and started packing everything that would fit. He grabbed the cash he had already earned and stuffed it at the very bottom of his socks and then pulled on his boots. He had to be gone before Pancho got back. He would lose out on a few days of pay, but better that than lose his life. He was ready to go, when he heard a knock on the bedroom door. He stuffed the bag in the closet and jumped into bed, pulling the covers over his body. "Come in," he said.

Lorena walked in, disturbed. She pulled the chair that was leaning against the wall and scooted it close to the bed. "There's something else. And this is it. I mean this is really it. This is why I'm telling you what Pancho's doing. I think you need to be prepared."

"What?" he said.

"It's been a long time since you've seen her." She paused, as if the words were too difficult. "Miguel, your mother is getting very senile."

"How senile?" he said, perking up.

"She forgets things sometimes. People sometimes. And . . ."

"What? What?"

"After your father disowned you—and she still doesn't believe the story."

"The story?"

"About you and that other boy. She doesn't believe it. None of us do."

"Uh, that's good."

"But after he disowned you, she never gave up on you. She knew she would see you again. She's been saving things for you. After your father died, he left, well, quite a bit of money."

"How much?"

"A lot, Miguel. You don't even have to work if you don't want. She's been saving it for you. I only tell you this because I want you to be prepared. I told Pancho it wasn't a good idea to not tell you first. But he was just so excited about the, you know, the . . . Well, he wants you to be happy."

"What if she doesn't recognize me?" he asked.

"She's senile. It just means we'd have to . . . What am I saying? She will."

Juan sat up on his bed. "Well, then, I'll look forward to meeting her. I mean, seeing her again."

Lorena left the room. Juan paced back and forth with a burst of energy. When he heard the truck pull up onto the gravel, he said to himself, "Here we go." He looked at himself in the mirror. He saw staring at him Miguel Valencia Godoy. Clean-shaven, handsome, lean-bodied, confident. But then he glimpsed something that bothered him, a dull gleam in his eyes, something that didn't belong to him. Insecurity. It was Juan. He shook it off and went out into the living room to see his mother.

# Komodo Dragon

RAY GONZALEZ

There is a Komodo dragon in my backyard. It has my cat in its mouth and chews it savagely as I appear on the porch. The Komodo is at least twelve feet long and larger than an alligator. When it swallows the cat, a cloud of hairs hangs in the air in front of its mighty face. The Komodo tramples through my mother's flowers and stops under our small willow tree. It looks up at the birdcage my mother hung on the willow for decoration. There are no birds in it, but the Komodo raises itself on its back legs and rips the wooden cage off the tree. The sound of snapping, crunching wood punctuates the morning. I come out of my shock and reach for the garden hose coiled on the porch. I don't know what else to do, so I turn it on full and spray the Komodo with a jet of water. It is twenty yards from me, but the water seems to work because it stops, its huge feet slowly sinking in the mud, the water ricocheting off its body. It closes its eyes and doesn't move because I think it loves the water! I stand there for minutes, spraying it and flooding the backyard. I want to drop the hose and run inside to call 911, but all I can do is wet this content creature. The Komodo has sunk low enough in the mud to swim. I keep the powerful jet of water on its head as I flood the yard. It seems to be the spot, but I have to really aim because the Komodo is floating away on the lake that has rapidly formed. It keeps its eyes shut as the water carries it across the yard, our flowers and nicely trimmed grass now a swamp. I grab the hose head with both hands because my wrist is getting sore, but I can't stop because this is working. The Komodo is a hypnotized mountain of muscle sailing toward the twisted and torn back gate, the place where it entered, and I hope it doesn't get caught in the metal. I descend the stairs with the hose, my nozzle pointing the way. The Komodo is asleep as it makes it through the gate, but the hose doesn't reach any farther. What do I do if it wakes up? The Komodo has come to a halt in the middle of the alley which is dry. I can't reach its head with the hose any longer, so I drop it and run. Before I reach the porch stairs, a screech of tires and the sounds of a heavy engine reverberate in the alley. I remember today is trash day. The crew calmly gets out of the truck and two guys with gloves lift the sleeping dragon by its head and tail, swing it a couple of times, then toss it high into the compactor. I yell, "Wait! Wait! That's a Komodo dragon!" The roar of the compactor drowns me out as they climb in and drive down the alley. I run to the gate as the truck halts by the street. It shakes and explodes and the compactor flies into pieces as this enormous Godzilla monster rises from the back, its enormous jaws foaming with crushed soda cans, styrofoam, and plastic bags full of my neighbor's trash. I run as the horrifying screams of the garbage crew echo down the alley.

# Pyramid

RAY GONZALEZ

I come out of the jungle and find the massive pyramid overgrown with vines. I have been searching for it for years, wasted several research grants traveling the Americas to find it, and here it is at last. I wipe sweat from my forehead with my hankie and behold the ancient brilliance. Most of the stairs have been worn down over the centuries and I don't think I can climb to the top. There are several strange markings on one wall. As a scholar of lost civilizations, I am familiar with most forgotten languages, but these petroglyphs are unknown to me. I am totally baffled at the way certain animals have been drawn around unusual letters and symbols. In one, what appears to be a crocodile is being prayed to by five kneeling men. In another area, large flying birds are holding bows and flinging arrows at running stick men. As I peer at these images through my sunglasses, a purple snake crawls toward the wall about ten feet away. I turn to make sure no more reptiles are at my feet, but don't see any. Within seconds, the purple snake disappears into a crack in the wall. It doesn't take long to hike completely around the pyramid and plan my course of action. I climb over fallen chunks of stone and trip over vines, but make it all the way around convinced this is the place to conduct my studies. I stop where I began, near the crack where the snake entered, and pull a can of spray paint from my knapsack. I draw bright orange letters on the pyramid. "Steve does it with Mary" on one wall. A couple of feet above that—"Wanna a good time? Call Fernie's mother," and I write her phone number in the dayglow orange. This goes on for almost one hour, the remote corner of the jungle leaving me alone to pronounce things—"Jito Gives Blow Jobs," "Rosaldo Was Here," even "Gringo Go Home." Soon, I run out of paint, but don't want to open another can. I step back and marvel at what I have done, pleased that I have not damaged a single ancient marking with the paint. Now, all I have to do is wait for my theories to be proven. I retreat into the jungle, pausing to make notes in my journal on how the purple snake may complicate things, then head to the canoe. When I reach the boat, the silent Talo, my Mayan guide, listens as I tell him this has been a very successful expedition.

# The Jalapeno Contest

RAY GONZALEZ

Freddy and his brother Tesoro have not seen each other in five years and
they sit at the kitchen table in Freddy's house and have a jalapeno contest.
A large bowl of big green and orange jalapeno peppers sits between the two
brothers. A saltshaker and two small glasses of beer accompany this feast.
When Tesoro nods his head, the two men begin to eat the raw jalapenos.
The goal is to see which man can eat the most peppers until the other one
quits. It is an old ritual from their father, but the two brothers tried it only
once years ago. Both quit after two peppers and laughed it off. This time,
things are different. They are older and want to prove a point. Freddy bites
his first one slower than Tesoro, who takes only two bites to finish his and
is now on his second. No one says anything, though a close study of each
man's face would tell you the sudden burst of jalapeno energy does not
waste time in changing the eater's perception of reality. Freddy works on his
second as Tesoro rips into his fourth. Freddy is already sweating from his
head and is surprised to see Tesoro's fat face has not changed its steady,
consuming look. His long, black hair is neatly combed and not one bead of
sweat has popped out. Tesoro is the first to sip from the beer before hitting
his fifth jalapeno. Freddy leans back as the table begins to sway in his damp
vision. He coughs and a sharp pain rips through his chest. Tesoro attempts
to laugh at his brother, but Freddy sees it is something else. As Freddy finishes his third pepper, Tesoro begins to breathe faster upon swallowing his
sixth jalapeno. The contest momentarily stops as both brothers shift in their
seats and the sweat pours down both their faces. Freddy clutches his stomach as he reaches for a fourth delight. Tesoro has not taken his seventh and
it is clear to Freddy his brother is suffering big time. There is a bright blue
bird sitting on Tesoro's head and Tesora is struggling to laugh because
Freddy has a huge red spider crawling on top of his head. Freddy wipes the
sweat from his eyes and finishes his fourth pepper. Tesoro sips more beer,
sprinkles salt on the tip of his jalapeno, and bites it down to the stem.
Freddy, who has not touched his beer, stares in amazement as two Tesoros
sit in front of him. They both rise hastily from the table, their beer guts
pushing it against Freddy, who leans back as the two Tesoros waver in the

kitchen light. Freddy hears a tremendous fart erupt from his brother, who sits down again. Freddy holds his fifth jalapeno and can't breathe. Tesoro's face is purple, but the blue bird has been replaced by a burning flame of light that weaves over Tesoro's shiny head. Freddy is convinced he is having a heart attack as he watches his brother fight for breath. Freddy bites into his fifth as Tesoro flips his eighth jalapeno into his mouth, stem and all. This is it. Freddy goes into convulsions and drops to the floor as he tries to reach for his glass of beer. He shakes on the dirty floor as the huge animal that is Tesoro pitches forward and throws up millions of jalapeno seeds all over the table. The last thing Freddy sees before he passes out is his brother's body levitating above the table. Freddy holds for one more second as an angel, dressed in green jalapeno robes, floats into the room, extends a hand to Tesoro and floats away with him. When Freddy wakes up minutes later, he tries to get up and make it to the bathroom before his body lets go through his pants. As he reaches the bathroom door, he turns and gazes upon the jalapeno plants growing healthy and large on the kitchen table, thick peppers hanging under their leaves, their branches immersed in the largest pile of yellow jalapeno seeds Freddy has ever seen.

# The Glass Eye

RAY GONZALEZ

Folio had a glass eye he loved to bounce on the floor. It would bounce higher than a basketball. He would sit on the sofa and bounce it. It would almost touch the light on the ceiling before coming down into his open hand. One day, as he was bouncing his glass eye, he heard a knock on the door. He quickly screwed the eye into his left socket and went to the door. When he opened it, he met a tall, thin woman who wore nothing but a yellow bikini. Folio blinked several times because the late fall air was chilly and he wondered how she could stand there like that. The woman had brown hair and a deep tan. She smiled at him without saying a word. Folio was not good with women, so he just stood there in his old sweater and sweatpants and stared. The woman's body reflected the cold as goose bumps rose all over her exposed skin. Folio stared at her small yet dominant breasts and her flat belly. She stood barefoot on the cold cement of the porch. Folio didn't know what to do because her sweet smile and red lips caught him. He noticed she held both hands behind her back, which helped her breasts reach closer to him. She extended her right hand to him. It held a tiny, white box. He took it from her tiny hand. Before he could look at her body again, the woman in the yellow bikini turned and ran from the porch. Folio panicked, but could not move. He thought he saw her get into a waiting van as he quickly shut the door. His old slippers scraped on the wooden floor as he went back to his trusted sofa. He sat down and carefully opened the tiny box. A glass eye stared up at him. It's eyeball was green. Folio's real eye and his artificial one were brown. He took the new eye and held it up to the light. He removed his left eye with a quick pinch of his fingers, then inserted the new one. He turned to the window beside the sofa and saw a woman standing outside, her face pressed to the glass. He rose, blinked, and realized it was the woman in the yellow bikini. Now, she was enormously fat and her breasts were huge. Folds of fat skin drew him to the window. It was the same woman. He knew it as she smiled at him and pointed to the door. Folio almost tripped on his untied slippers as he ran to it. He swung the door open and the fat woman flew into his arms. As they hugged, Folio's artificial eye flew out of his hand and bounced loudly across the floor. He tried to turn, but the perfumed body of the huge woman kept him from seeing where the eye landed. They pushed each other toward the sofa as Folio heard the glass eye roll somewhere in the hidden shadows of his living room.

# Mistakes

RAY GONZALEZ

Henry made the mistake of walking in on David and Lencha, his girlfriend. They were doing it on the floor and Henry made the mistake of forgetting there was a full moon that night. He made the wrong choice of grabbing the naked David and tossing him through the open window. The guy landed in the rosebushes and never came back. Henry made the error of forgiving Lencha, whom he never trusted again, though she never knew about Henry and Sophie. They both made the same mistake. Henry was in error when he quit his job as a car mechanic and went to work for Heavy Sanchez, his old buddy from high school. Before Henry knew it, he had taken the wrong path by making too much money pushing coke. His new car and clothes caught the attention of the guys in the suits who followed him all the time. Henry spoke words he shouldn't have on his cell phone and let the suits know where he was meeting Lencha's father, who did not choose wisely by liking his daughter's boyfriend too much. That night, Henry made a wrong turn getting to the rendevous near Copia and Alameda streets and was late. The suits thought everyone was there and busted several guys, including Lencha's father, but Henry was busy making a U-turn near the railroad tracks and missed the bust by three minutes. He drove inaccurately by turning into a dark alley when he spotted the police cars, but it was a dead end and he had to stop between narrow brick walls covered in graffiti. He got out of the car and took a peek around the corner at the police action. It was one block down and he couldn't tell who got busted. As he huddled in the shadows, he was dressed in the wrong clothes because four dudes appeared out of nowhere and jumped him. Henry decided to fight back with his kick-boxing lessons and took two of them down before making the untaught move of slipping and falling. As he went down, the gun in his pants went off and killed the third homeboy as the fourth ran. Henry hurried to his car and jumped in, but the gunshot drew the attention of the suits, who were almost done with their bust. They chose the tactical error of getting to the alley too late because Henry was gone, his panic giving him the skill to drive his car out of the alley in reverse. Henry lay low for a while, but selected to think with his dick instead of his brain and went to bed with Marina,

David's ex. The hidden video camera caught everything, but the guy who set it up for David read the instructions incorrectly and placed the camera lens at an angle that caught close-ups of the lovers' asses, not their faces. Henry never found out about it because he never saw Marina again, deciding to leave town instead. He ran around Los Angeles for a few weeks, trying to connect with cool people. When he found the right circle of friends and started delivering stuff again, he was the last-minute substitute driver for a key delivery to a very rich and powerful client who made the mistake of paying thousands in cash before seeing the goods. Henry worked at night for his new boss, but this client only did business during the day and the regular day driver was out sick. Being new to southern California, Henry got lost on the way to the rendezvous with the client, jumped on the Santa Ana freeway, a faster route he rarely took. Part of the freeway collapsed and it took two days to find the remains of Henry's car under the concrete, his body smashed so flat it was hard to pick the bones from the forty pounds of cocaine spread all over the wreckage like a white cloud sending Henry to heaven. By the way, his boss made the mistake of creating the impression he thought it was cool to rip people off, because he was shot dead in his elegant home the day after one of the largest earthquakes in modern history hit L.A.

# Birthmates

GISH JEN

This was what responsibility meant in a dinosaur industry, toward the end of yet another quarter of bad-to-worse news: that you called the travel agent back, and even though there was indeed an economy room in the hotel where the conference was being held, a room overlooking the cooling towers, you asked if there wasn't something still cheaper. And when Marie-the-new-girl came back with something amazingly cheap, you took it— only to discover, as Art Woo was discovering now, that the doors were locked after nine o'clock. The neighborhood had looked not great but not bad, and the building itself, regular enough. Brick, four stories, a rolled-up awning. A bright-lit hotel logo, with a raised-plastic, smiling sun. But there was a kind of crossbar rigged across the inside of the glass door, and that was not at all regular. A two-by-four, it appeared, wrapped in rust-colored carpet. Above this, inside the glass, hung a small gray sign. If the taxi had not left, Art might not have rung the buzzer, as per the instructions.

But the taxi had indeed left, and the longer Art huddled on the stoop in the clumpy December snow, the emptier and more poorly lit the street appeared. His buzz was answered by an enormous black man wearing a neck brace. The shoulder seams of the man's blue waffle-weave jacket were visibly straining; around the brace was tied a necktie, which reached only a third of the way down his chest. All the same, it was neatly fastened together with a hotel-logo tie tack about two inches from the bottom. The tie tack was smiling; the man was not. He held his smooth, round face perfectly expressionless, and he lowered his gaze at every opportunity—not so that it was rude, but so that it was clear he wasn't selling anything to anybody. Regulation tie, thought Art. Regulation jacket. He wondered if the man would turn surly soon enough.

For Art had come to few conclusions about life in his forty-nine years, but this was one of them: that men turned surly when their clothes didn't fit them. This man, though, belied the rule. He was courteous, almost formal in demeanor; and if the lobby seemed not only too small for him, like his jacket, but also too much like a bus station, what with its smoked mirror wall, and its linoleum, and its fake wood, and its vending machines, what did that matter to Art? The sitting area looked as though it was in the process of being cleaned; the sixties Scandinavian chairs and couch and coffee table had been pulled every which way, as if by someone hell-bent on the dust balls. Still Art proceeded with his check-in. He was going with his gut, here as in any business situation. Here as in any business situation, he was looking foremost at the personnel, and the man with the neck brace had put him at some ease. It wasn't until after Art had taken his credit card back that he noticed, above the checkout desk, a wooden plaque from a neighborhood association. He squinted at its brass faceplate:

FEWEST CUSTOMER INJURIES, 1972–73.

What about the years since '73? Had the hotel gotten more dangerous, or had other hotels gotten safer? Maybe neither. For all he knew, the neighborhood association had dissolved and was no longer distributing plaques. Art reminded himself that in life, some signs were no signs. It's what he used to tell his ex-wife, Lisa. Lisa, who loved to read everything into everything; Lisa, who was attuned. She left him on a day when she saw a tree get split by lightning. Of course, that was an extraordinary thing to see. An event of a lifetime. Lisa said the tree had sizzled. He wished he had seen it, too. But what did it mean, except that the tree had been the tallest in the neighborhood, and was no longer? It meant nothing; ditto for the plaque. Art made his decision, which perhaps was not the right decision. Perhaps he should have looked for another hotel.

But it was late—on the way out, his plane had sat on the runway, just sat and sat, as if it were never going to take off—and God only knew what he would have ended up paying if he had relied on a cabbie simply to take him somewhere else. Forget twice—it could have been three, four times what he would have paid for that room with the view of the cooling towers, easy. At this hour, after all, and that was a conference rate.

So he double-locked his door instead. He checked behind the hollow-core doors of the closet, and under the steel-frame bed, and also in the swirly-green shower-stall unit. He checked behind the seascapes to be sure there weren't any peepholes. The window opened onto a fire escape; not much he could do about that except check the window locks. Big help that those were—a sure deterrent for the subset of all burglars that was burglars too skittish to break glass. Which was what percent of intruders, probably? Ten percent? Fifteen? He closed the drapes, then decided he would be more comfortable with the drapes open. He wanted to be able to see what approached, if anything did. He unplugged the handset of his phone from the base, a calculated risk. On the one hand, he wouldn't be able to call the police if there was an intruder. On the other, he would be armed. He had read somewhere a story about a woman who threw the handset of her phone at an attacker and killed him. Needless to say, there had been some luck involved in that eventuality. Still, Art thought that (a) surely he could throw as hard as that woman, and (b) even without the luck, his throw would most likely be hard enough to slow up an intruder at least. Especially since this was an old handset, the hefty kind that made you feel the seriousness of human communication. In a newer hotel, he probably would have had a lighter phone, with lots of buttons he would never use but which would make him feel he had many resources at his disposal. In the conference hotel, there were probably buttons for the health club, and for the concierge, and for the three restaurants, and for room service. He tried not to think about this as he went to sleep, clutching the handset.

He did not sleep well.

In the morning, he debated whether to take the handset with him into the elevator. It wasn't like a knife, say, that could be whipped out of nowhere. Even a pistol at least fit in a guy's pocket. A telephone handset did not. All the same, he took it with him. He tried to carry it casually, as if he were going out for a run and using it for a hand weight, or as if he were in the telephone business.

He strode down the hail. Victims shuffled; that's what everybody said. A lot of mugging had to do with nonverbal cues, which is why Lisa used to walk tall after dark, sending vibes. For this, he used to tease her. If she was so worried, she should lift weights and run, the way he did. That, he maintained, was the substantive way of helping oneself. She had agreed. For a while they had met after work at the gym. Then she dropped a weight on her toe and decided she preferred to sip piña coladas and watch. Naturally, he grunted on. But to what avail? Who could appreciate his pectorals through his suit and overcoat? Pectorals had no deterrent value, that was what he was thinking now. And he was, though not short, not tall. He continued striding. Sending vibes. He was definitely going to eat in the dining room of the hotel where the conference was being held, he decided. What's more, he was going to have a full American breakfast with bacon and eggs, none of this continental bullshit.

In truth, he had always considered the sight of men eating croissants slightly ridiculous, especially at the beginning, when for the first bite they had to maneuver the point of the crescent into their mouths. No matter what a person did, he ended up with an asymmetrical mouthful of pastry, which he then had to relocate with his tongue to a more central location. This made him look less purposive than he might. Also, croissants were more apt than other breakfast foods to spray little flakes all over one's clean dark suit. Art himself had accordingly never ordered a croissant in any working situation, and he believed that attention to this sort of detail was how it was that he had not lost his job like so many of his colleagues.

This was, in other words, how it happened that he was still working in a dying industry, and was now carrying a telephone handset with him into the elevator. Art braced himself as the elevator doors opened slowly, jerkily, in the low-gear manner of elevator doors in the Third World. He strode in, and was surrounded by, of all things, children. Down in the lobby, too, there were children and, here and there, women he knew to be mothers by their looks of dogged exasperation. A welfare hotel! He laughed out loud. Almost everyone was black; the white children stood out like little missed opportunities of the type that made Art's boss throw his tennis racket across the room. Of course, the racket was always in its padded protective cover and not in much danger of getting injured, though the person in whose vicinity it was aimed sometimes was. Art once suffered what he rather hoped would turn out to be a broken nose, but it was only a bone bruise. There was so little skin discoloration that people had a hard time believing the incident had actually taken place. Yet it had. *Don't talk to me about fault. Bottom line, it's you Japs who are responsible for this whole fucking mess,* his boss had said. Never mind that what was the matter with minicomputers, really, was personal computers, a wholly American phenomenon. And never mind that Art could have sued over this incident if he could have proved that it had happened. Some people, most notably Lisa, thought he at least ought to have quit.

But he didn't sue and he didn't quit. He took his tennis racket on the nose, so to speak, and when his boss apologized the next day for losing control, Art said he understood. And when his boss said that Art shouldn't take what he said personally—that he knew Art was not a Jap, but a Chink, plus he had called someone else a lazy Wop that very morning, it was just his style—Art said again that he understood, and also that he hoped his boss would remember Art's great understanding come promotion time. Which his boss did, to Art's satisfaction. In Art's view, this was a victory. In Art's view, he had made a deal out of the incident. He had perceived leverage where others would only have perceived affront. He had maintained a certain perspective.

But this certain perspective was, in addition to the tree, why Lisa had left him. He thought of that now, the children underfoot, his handset in hand. So many children. It was as if he were seeing before him all the children he would never have. His heart lost muscle. A child in a red running suit ran by, almost grabbed the handset out of Art's grasp. Then another, in a brown jacket with a hood. Art looked up. A group of grade-school boys was arrayed about the seating area, watching. Art had become the object of a dare, apparently; realizing this, he felt renewed enough to want to laugh again. When a particularly small child swung by in his turn—a child of maybe five or six, small enough to be wearing snow pants—Art almost tossed the handset to him. But who wanted to be charged for a missing phone?

As it was, Art wondered if he shouldn't put the handset back in his room rather than carry it around all day. For what was he going to do at the hotel where the conference was, check it? He imagined himself running into Billy Shore—that was his counterpart at Info-Edge, and his competitor in the insurance market. A man with no management ability, and no technical background, either, but he could offer customers a personal computer option, which Art could not. What's more, Billy had been a quarterback in college. This meant he strutted around as though it still mattered that he had connected with his tight end in the final minutes of what Art could not help but think of as the Wilde-Beastie game. And it meant that Billy was sure to ask him, *What are you doing with a phone in your hand? Talking to yourself again?* Making everyone around them laugh.

Billy was that kind of guy. He had come up through sales, and was always cracking a certain type of joke—about drinking, or sex, or how much the wife shopped. Of course, he never used those words. He never called things by their plain names. He always talked in terms of *knocking back some brewskis*, or *running the triple option*, or *doing some damage*. He made assumptions as though it were a basic bodily function. Of course his knowledge was the common knowledge. Of course people understood what it was that he was referring to so delicately. *Listen, champ*, he said, putting his arm around you. If he was smug, it was in an affable kind of way. *So what do you think the poor people are doing tonight?* Billy not only spoke what Art called Mainstreamese, he spoke such a pure dialect of it that Art once asked him if he realized he was a pollster's delight. He spoke the thoughts of thousands, Art told him; he breathed their very words. Naturally, Billy did not respond, except to say, *What's that?* and turn away. He rubbed his torso as he turned, as if ruffling his chest hairs through the long-staple cotton. Primate behavior, Lisa used to call this. It was her belief that neckties evolved in order to check this very motion, uncivilized as it was. She also believed that this was the sort of thing you never saw Asian men do—at least not if they were brought up properly.

Was that true? Art wasn't so sure. Lisa had grown up on the West Coast. She was full of Asian consciousness, whereas all he knew was that no one had so much as smiled politely at his pollster remark. On the other hand, the first time Art was introduced to Billy, and Billy said, *Art Woo, how's that for a nice Pole-ack name*, everyone broke right up in great rolling guffaws. Of course, they laughed the way people laughed at conferences, which was not because something was really funny, but because it was part of being a good guy, and because they didn't want to appear to have missed their cue.

The phone, the phone. If only Art could fit it in his briefcase! But his briefcase was overstuffed; it was always overstuffed; really, it was too bad he had the slim silhouette type, and hard-sided besides. Italian. That was Lisa's doing; she thought the fatter kind made him look like a salesman. Not that there was anything the matter with that, in his view. Billy Shore notwithstanding, sales were important. But she was the liberal arts type, Lisa was, the type who did not like to think about money, but only about her feelings. Money was not money to her, but support, and then a means of support much inferior to hand-holding or other forms of fingerplay. She did not believe in a modern-day economy, in which everyone played a part in a large and complex whole that introduced efficiencies that at least theoretically raised everyone's standard of living. She believed in expressing herself. Also in taking classes, and in knitting. There was nothing, she believed, like taking a walk in the autumn woods wearing a hand-knit sweater. Of course, she did look beautiful in them, especially the violet ones. That was her color—Asians are winters, she always said—and sometimes she liked to wear the smallest smidgen of matching violet eyeliner.

Little Snowpants ran at Art again, going for the knees. A tackle, thought Art as he went down. Red Running Suit snatched away the handset and went sprinting off, trimphant. Teamwork! The children chortled together. How could Art not smile, even if they had gotten his overcoat dirty? He brushed himself off, ambled over.

"Hey, guys," he said. "That was some move back there."

"Ching chong polly wolly wing wong," said Little Snowpants.

"Now, now, that's no way to talk," said Art.

"Go to hell!" said Brown Jacket, pulling at the corners of his eyes to make them slanty.

"Listen up," said Art. "I'll make you a deal." Really he only meant to get the handset back, so as to avoid getting charged for it.

But the next thing he knew, something had hit his head with a crack, and he was out.

Lisa had left in a more or less amicable way. She had not called a lawyer, or a mover. She had simply pressed his hands with both of hers and, in her most California voice, said, *Let's be nice.* Then she had asked him if he wouldn't help her move her boxes, at least the heavy ones. He had helped. He had carried the heavy boxes, and also the less heavy ones. Being a weight lifter, after all. He had sorted books and rolled glasses into pieces of newspaper, feeling all the while like a statistic. A member of the modern age, a story for their friends to rake over, and all because he had not gone with Lisa to her grieving group. Or at least that was the official beginning of the trouble. Probably the real beginning had been when Lisa—no, *they*—had trouble getting pregnant. When they decided to, as the saying went, do infertility. Or had he done the deciding, as Lisa later maintained? He had thought it was a joint decision, though it was true that he had done the analysis that led to the joint decision. He had been the one to figure the odds, to do the projections. He had drawn the decision tree according to whose branches they had nothing to lose by going ahead.

Neither one of them had realized how much would be involved—the tests, the procedures, the drugs, the ultrasounds. Lisa's arms were black and blue from having her blood drawn every day, and before long he was giving practice shots to an orange, that he might prick her some more. Then he was telling her to take a breath so that on the exhale he could poke her in the buttocks. This was nothing like poking an orange. The first time, he broke out in such a sweat that his vision blurred; he pulled the needle out slowly and crookedly, occasioning a most unorangelike cry. The second time, he wore a sweatband. Her ovaries swelled to the point where he could feel them through her jeans.

Art still had the used syringes—snapped in half and stored, as per their doctor's recommendation, in plastic soda bottles. Lisa had left him those. Bottles of medical waste, to be disposed of responsibly, meaning that he was probably stuck with them, ha-ha, for the rest of his life. This was his souvenir of their ordeal. Hers was sweeter—a little pile of knit goods. For through it all, she had knit, as if to demonstrate an alternative use of needles. Sweaters, sweaters, but also baby blankets, mostly to give away, only one or two to keep. She couldn't help herself. There was anesthesia and egg harvesting, and anesthesia and implanting, until she finally did get pregnant, twice. The third time, she went to four and a half months before the doctors found a problem. On the amnio, it showed up, brittle-bone disease—a genetic abnormality such as could happen to anyone.

He steeled himself for another attempt; she grieved. And this was the difference between them, that he saw hope, still, some feeble, skeletal hope, where she saw loss. She called the fetus her baby, though it was not a baby, just a baby-to-be, as he tried to say; as even the grieving-group facilitator tried to say. Lisa said Art didn't understand, couldn't possibly understand. She said it was something you understood with your body, and that it was not his body, but hers, which knew the baby, loved the baby, lost the baby. In the grieving class, the women agreed. They commiserated. They bonded, subtly affirming their common biology by doing 85 percent of the talking. The room was painted mauve—a feminine color that seemed to support them in their process. At times, it seemed that the potted palms were female, too, nodding, nodding, though really their sympathy was just rising air from the heating vents. Other husbands started missing sessions—they never talked anyway, you hardly noticed their absence—and finally he missed some also. One, maybe two, for real reasons, nothing cooked up. But the truth was, as Lisa sensed, that he thought she had lost perspective. They could try again, after all. What did it help to despair? Look, they knew they could get pregnant and, what's more, sustain the pregnancy. That was progress. But she was like an island in her grief—a retreating island, if there was such a thing, receding toward the horizon of their marriage, and then to its vanishing point.

Of course, he had missed her terribly at first. Now he missed her still, but more sporadically, at odd moments—for example, now, waking up in a strange room with ice on his head. He was lying on an unmade bed just like the bed in his room, except that everywhere around it were heaps of what looked to be blankets and clothes. The only clothes on a hanger were his jacket and overcoat; these hung neatly, side by side, in the otherwise-empty closet. There was also an extra table in this room, with a two-burner hotplate, a pan on top of that, and a pile of dishes. A brown cube refrigerator. The drapes were closed. A chair had been pulled up close to him; the bedside light was on. A woman was leaning into its circle, mopping his brow.

"Don't you move, now," she said.

She was the shade of black Lisa used to call mochaccino, and she was wearing a blue flowered apron. Kind eyes; a long face—the kind of face where you could see the muscles of the jaw working alongside the cheekbone. An upper lip like an archery bow; a graying Afro, shortish. She smelled of smoke. Nothing unusual except that she was so very thin, about the thinnest person he had ever seen, and yet she was cooking something—burning something, it seemed, though maybe the smell was just a hair fallen onto the heating element. She stood up to tend the pan. The acrid smell faded. He saw powder on the table. White; there was a plastic bag full of it. His eyes widened. He sank back, trying to figure out what to do. His head pulsed. Tylenol, he needed, two. Lisa always took one because she was convinced the dosages recommended were based on large male specimens, and though she had never said that she thought he ought to keep it to one also, not being so tall, he was adamant about taking two. Two, two, two. He wanted his drugs; he wanted them now. And his own drugs, that was, not somebody else's.

"Those kids kind of rough," said the woman. "They getting to that age. I told them one of these days somebody gonna get hurt, and sure enough, they knocked you right out. You might as well been hit with a bowling ball. I never saw anything like it. We called the Man, but they got other things on their mind besides to come see about trouble here. Nobody shot, so they went on down to the Dunkin' Donuts. They know they can count on a ruckus there." She winked. "How you feelin? That egg hurt?"

He felt his head. A lump sat right on top of it, incongruous as something left by a glacier. What were those called, those stray boulders you saw perched in hair-raising positions? On cliffs? He thought.

"I feel like I died and came back to life headfirst," he said.

"I gonna make you something nice. Make you feel a whole lot better."

"Uh," said Art. "If you don't mind, I'd rather just have a Tylenol. You got any Tylenol? I had some in my briefcase. If I still have my briefcase."

"Your what?"

"My briefcase," said Art again, with a panicky feeling. "Do you know what happened to my briefcase?"

"Oh, it's right by the door. I'll get it, don't move."

Then there it was, his briefcase, its familiar hard-sided Italian slenderness resting right on his stomach. He clutched it. "Thank you," he whispered.

"You need help with that thing?"

"No," said Art. But when he opened the case, it slid, and everything spilled out—his notes, his files, his papers. All that figuring. How strange his concerns looked on this brown shag carpet.

"Here," said the woman. And again—"I'll get it, don't move"— as gently, beautifully, she gathered up all the folders and put them in the case. There was an odd, almost practiced finesse to her movements; the files could have been cards in a card dealer's hands. "I used to be a nurse," she explained, as if reading his mind. "I picked up a few folders in my time. Here's the Tylenol."

"I'll have two."

"Course you will," she said. "Two Tylenol and some hot milk with honey. Hope you don't mind the powdered. We just got moved here, we don't have no supplies. I used to be a nurse, but I don't got no milk and I don't got no Tylenol, my guests got to bring their own. How you like that."

Art laughed as much as he could. "You got honey, though. How's that?"

"I don't know, it got left here by somebody," said the nurse. "Hope there's nothing growing in it."

Art laughed again, then let her help him sit up to take his pills. The nurse—her name was Cindy—plumped his pillows. She administered his milk. Then she sat—very close to him, it seemed—and chatted amiably about this and that. How she wasn't going to be staying at the hotel for too long, how her kids had had to switch schools, how she wasn't afraid to take in a strange, injured man. After all, she grew up in the projects; she could take care of herself. She showed him her switchblade, which had somebody's initials carved on it, she didn't know whose. She had never used it, she said, somebody gave it to her. And that somebody didn't know whose initials those were, either, she said, at least so far as she knew. Then she lit a cigarette and smoked while he told her first about his conference and then about how he had ended up at this hotel by mistake. He told her the latter with some hesitation, hoping he wasn't offending her. She laughed with a cough, emitting a series of smoke puffs.

"Sure musta been a shock," she said. "End up in a place like this. This ain't no place for a nice boy like you."

That stung a little, being called *boy*. But more than the stinging, he felt something else. "What about you? It's no place for you, either, you and your kids."

"Maybe so," she said. "But that's how the Almighty planned it, right? You folk rise up while we set and watch." She said this with so little rancor, with something so like intimacy, that it almost seemed an invitation of sorts.

Maybe he was kidding himself. Maybe he was assuming things, just like Billy Shore, just like men throughout the ages. Projecting desire where there was none, assigning and imagining, and in juicy detail. Being Asian didn't exempt him from that. *You folk.*

Art was late, but it didn't much matter. His conference was being held in conjunction with a much larger conference, the real draw; the idea being that maybe between workshops and on breaks, the conferees would drift down and see what minicomputers could do for them. That mostly meant lunch, which probably would be slow at best. In the meantime, things were totally dead, allowing Art to appreciate just how much the trade-show floor had shrunk—down to a fraction of what it had been in previous years, and the booths were not what they had been, either. It used to be that the floor was crammed with the fanciest booths on the market. Art's was twenty by twenty; it took days to put together. Now you saw blank spots on the floor where exhibitors didn't even bother to show up, and those weren't even as demoralizing as some of the makeshift jobbies—exhibit booths that looked like high school science-fair projects. They might as well have been made out of cardboard and Magic Marker. Art himself had a booth you could buy from an airplane catalog, the kind that rolled up into Cordura bags. And people were stingy with brochures now, too. Gone were the twelve-page, four-color affairs. Now the pamphlets were four-page, two-color, with extrabold graphics for attempted pizzazz, and not everybody got one, only people who were serious.

Art set up. Then, even though he should have been manning his spot, he drifted from booth to booth, saying hello to people he should have seen at breakfast. They were happy to see him, to talk shop, to pop some grapes off the old grapevine. Really, if he hadn't been staying in a welfare hotel, he would have felt downright respected. *You folk.* What folk did Cindy mean? Maybe she was just being matter-of-fact, keeping her perspective. Although how could anyone be so matter-of-fact about something so bitter? He wondered this even as he imagined taking liberties with her. These began with a knock on her door and coursed through some hot times but finished (what a good boy he was) with him rescuing her and her children (he wondered how many there were) from their dead-end life. What was the matter with him, that he could not imagine mating without legal sanction? His libido was not what it should be, clearly, or at least it was not what Billy Shore's was. Art tried to think *game plan*, but in truth he could not even identify what a triple option would be in this case. All he knew was that, assuming, to begin with, that she was willing, he couldn't sleep with a woman like Cindy and then leave her flat. She could *you folk* him; he could never *us folk* her.

He played with some software at a neighboring booth. It appeared interesting enough but kept crashing, so he couldn't tell much. Then he dutifully returned to his own booth, where he was visited by a number of people he knew, people with whom he was friendly—the sort of people to whom he might have shown pictures of his children. He considered telling one or two of them about the events of the morning. Not about the invitation that might not have been an invitation, but about finding himself in a welfare hotel and being beaned with his own telephone. Phrases drifted through his head. *Not as bad as you'd think. You'd be surprised how friendly. And how unpretentious. Though, of course, no health club.* But in the end, the subject simply did not come up and did not come up, until he realized that he was keeping it to himself, and that he was committing more resources to this task than he had readily available. He felt invaded—as if he had been infected by a self-replicating bug. Something that was iterating and iterating, crowding the cpu. The secret was intolerable; it was bound to spill out of him sooner or later. He just hoped it wouldn't be sooner. He just hoped it wouldn't be to Billy Shore, for whom Art had begun to search, so as to be certain to avoid him.

Art had asked about Billy at the various booths, but no one had seen him; his absence spooked Art. When finally some real live conferees stopped by to see his wares, Art had trouble concentrating. Everywhere in the conversation he was missing opportunities, he knew it. And all because his cpu was full of iterating nonsense. Not too long ago, in looking over some database software in which were loaded certain fun facts about people in the industry, Art had looked up Billy, and discovered that he had been born the same day Art was, only four years later. It just figured that Billy would be younger. That was irritating. But Art was happy for the information, too. He had made a note of it, so that when he ran into Billy at this conference, he could kid him about their birthdays. Now, he rehearsed. *Have I got a surprise for you. I always knew you were a Leo. I believe this makes us birthmates.* Anything not to mention the welfare hotel and all that had happened there.

In the end, Art did not run into Billy at all. In the end, Art wondered about Billy all day, only to learn, finally, that Billy had moved on to a new job in the Valley, with a start-up. In personal computers, naturally. A good move, no matter what kind of beating he took on his house.

"Life is about the long term," said Ernie Ford, the informant. "And let's face it, there is no long term here."

Art agreed as warmly as he could. In one way, he was delighted that his competitor had left. If nothing else, that would mean a certain amount of disarray at Info-Edge, which was good news for Art. The insurance market was, unfortunately, some 40 percent of his business, and he could use any advantage he could get. Another bonus was that Art was never going to have to see Billy again. Billy his birthmate, with his jokes and his Mainstreamese. Still, Art felt depressed.

"We should all have gotten out way before this," he said.

"Truer words were never spoke," said Ernie. Ernie had never been a particular friend of Art's, but talking about Billy was somehow making him chummier. "I'd have packed my bags by now if it weren't for the wife, the kids—they don't want to leave their friends, you know? Plus, the oldest is a junior in high school. We can't afford for him to move now. He's got to stay put and make those nice grades so he can make a nice college. That means I've got to stay, if it means pushing McMuffins for Ronald McDonald. But now you . . ."

"Maybe I should go," said Art.

"Definitely, you should go," said Ernie. "What's keeping you?"

"Nothing," said Art. "I'm divorced now. And that's that, right? Sometimes people get undivorced, but you can't exactly count on it."

"Go," said Ernie. "Take my advice. If I hear of anything, I'll send it your way."

"Thanks," said Art.

But of course he did not expect that Ernie would likely turn anything up soon. It had been a long time since anyone had called Art or anybody else he knew of. Too many people had gotten stranded, and they were too desperate, everybody knew it. Also, the survivors were looked upon with suspicion. Anybody who was any good had jumped ship early, that was the conventional wisdom. There was Art, struggling to hold on to his job, only to discover that there were times you didn't want to hold on to your job— times you ought to maneuver for the golden parachute and jump. Times the goal was to get yourself fired. Who would have figured that?

A few warm-blooded conferees at the end of the day—at least they were polite. Then, as he was packing up to return to the hotel, a surprise. A headhunter approached him, a friend of Ernest's, he said.

"Ernest?" said Art. "Oh, Ernie! Ford! Of course!"

The headhunter was a round, ruddy man with a ring of hair like Saint Francis of Assisi, and, sure enough, a handful of bread crumbs. A great opportunity, he said. Right now he had to run, but he knew just the guy Art had to meet, a guy who was coming in that evening. For something else, it happened, but he also needed someone like Art. Needed him yesterday, really. Should've been a priority. Might just be a match. Maybe a quick breakfast in the A.M.? Could he call in an hour or so? Art said, Of course. And when Saint Francis asked his room number, Art hesitated, but then gave the name of the welfare hotel. How would Saint Francis know what kind of hotel it was? Art gave the name out confidently, making his manner count. He almost hadn't made it to the conference at all, he said. Being so busy. It was only at the last minute that he realized he could do it. Things moved around, he found an opening and figured what the hell. But it was too late to book the conference hotel. Hence he was staying elsewhere.

Success. All day Art's mind had been churning; suddenly it seemed to empty. He might as well have been Billy, born on the same day as Art was, but in another year, under different stars. How much simpler things seemed. He did not labor on two, three, six tasks at once, multiprocessing. He knew one thing at a time, and that thing just now was that the day was a victory. He walked briskly back to the hotel. He crossed the lobby in a no-nonsense manner. An impervious man. He did not knock on Cindy's door. He was moving on, moving west. There would be a good job there, and a new life. Perhaps he would take up tennis. Perhaps he would own a Jacuzzi. Perhaps he would learn to like all those peculiar foods people ate out there, like jicama, and seaweed. Perhaps he would go macrobiotic.

It wasn't until he got to his room that he remembered that his telephone had no handset.

He sat on his bed. There was a noise at his window, followed, sure enough, by someone's shadow. He wasn't even surprised.

Anyway, the fellow wasn't stopping at Art's room, at least not on this trip. That was luck. *You folk*, Cindy had said, taking back the ice bag. Art could see her perspective; he was luckier than she, by far. But just now, as the shadow crossed his window again, he thought mostly about how unarmed he was. If he had a telephone, he would probably call Lisa—that was how big a pool seemed to be forming around him, all of a sudden; an ocean, it seemed. Also, he would call the police. But first he would call Lisa, and see how she felt about his possibly moving west. *Quite possibly*, he would say, not wanting to make it sound as though he was calling her for nothing—not wanting to make it sound as though he was awash, at sea, perhaps drowning. He would not want to sound like a haunted man; he would not want to sound as though he was calling from a welfare hotel, years too late, to say *Yes, that was a baby we had together, it would have been a baby.* For he could not help now but recall the doctor explaining about that child, a boy, who had appeared so mysteriously perfect in the ultrasound. Transparent, he had looked, and gelatinous, all soft head and quick heart; but he would have, in being born, broken every bone in his body.

# I Know What You Did Last Summer

MICHELE SERROS

The following is based on the actual diary of a twenty-seven-year-old Chicana Lollapalooza Road Poet.

It is not a definitive statement on the middle-class, alternative-music scene. It does not offer any solutions.

It is, however, a highly personal chronicle and may provide insight into the complicated world we live in.

Names, dates, and places have been changed in accordance with the wishes of those concerned.

Dear Diary,

I can't believe I was picked! Two months from now I will be on the road, touring with Lollapalooza. Yay! Beth says they were supposed to have Nirvana, but since they couldn't make it (sad), they will now do the spoken-word thing. Unknown poets instead of Nirvana, I don't see the connection. Anyway, who cares. I get to go on the road! I get to read my poetry to stadium crowds across the country and guess what? I will get paid! Can you believe it? I will keep a record of the whole experience and then I will have documentation of all my exciting adventures. Oh, but what if someone finds you? Oh God, dear diary, that could be hell. Some people just don't have the respect for other people's privacy. I guess I could use code names. Like symbols or maybe write everyone's name backward. No, I'll use no names, just like in *Go Ask Alice*. Then, in case someone finds you, my dear sweet best friend, they won't know I'm writing about them and then shun me like Harriet the Spy. Beth, oops, I mean ———— says she thinks the Beastie Boys are gonna be on this tour. I hope so. That ———— is so cute. This is gonna be the best summer of my life!

Dear Diary,

July 4 ———— today was the first day of the tour. We were in Las Vegas and it was 117 degrees. Can you believe it? I saw two boys faint outside of the mist tents. Part of my job as a Road Poet is to read poetry all the time, anytime. The heat was so painfully uncomfortable. . . . I changed three times cuz my clothes were just saturated with sweat. So, twelve of us will tour as Road Poets, but when we get to a new city, local poets will be added to that venue. One of the perks as a Road Poet is getting to eat for free at any of the food stands and ———— from Big Belly Burritos told me to come by anytime for free food. I asked him if there was lard in the burritos and he said no way and then when I said oh that's too bad, he laughed and said he'd throw in some lard just for me. He's pretty cute. If only he wasn't working a food stand.

Dear Diary, (Denver)
Every night ———— comes by the buses to deliver a stack of cheese pizzas and cases of beer. And sometimes ————, who's hanging with the Beasties, comes by with a chunk of pot the size of a brick and this is like eleven P.M. every night! I'm not even eating or smoking any of it. I want to stay in shape, I want to stay focused 'cause I have a lot of work ahead of me and I want to do a good job.

Dear Diary, (Kansas City)
Today was the greatest day. Hey, I sound like ———— from the Smashing Pumpkins! How can I not? I hear that song every single night before getting into this bunk to fall asleep into sweet nothingness. There are ten of us on this bus and it's really like a slumber party every night. We crank up the tunes, flash the hallway light off and on, and dance in the back end of the bus. All the other poets are so fun and nice. Today ———— helped me cut pieces of flannel for my "Grunge on a Stick." What I've done is taken Gene's old flannel shirts (one green, one brown) and cut them into one-inch squares. I skewer them on a bamboo stick and then roll a whole bunch of Teen Spirit (Baby Powder Soft scent) all over on them and then I sell them for twenty-five cents each. All these Midwest kids are buying them up! They always ask why some are green and some are brown and I just tell them, "Well, legally I can't say, but if I were you, I'd buy the green one." Ha, ha, ha! I got them believing they're ————'s old flannels when ———— gave them all away after his suicide. Anyway, today I sold a book! Can you believe it? This girl actually gave me six bucks for my book! I mean, she could have bought a hemp bag or a beaded choker or even a Big Belly Burrito, but no, she bought my book. This is going to be the best summer! See ya!

Dear Diary, (St. Paul)

What a horrible day. Today I read poems to only two people in the poetry corner and they weren't really in the corner to listen to poetry, but were just waiting to use the Porta Potti. They always put the outhouses by the poetry corner, so there's all these people who aren't into poetry and who just gotta take a piss and sometimes they yell things. It's sorta demeaning to be reading in a place called "the corner." I mean, why can't it be called "the stage," or "the arena," or even "the space"? "Corner" sounds so infantile and unprofessional. Being in a corner reminds me of school when I was sent to stand once cuz I talked too much and I had to stand in it to learn how to be quiet. Ugh. Anyway, there were these guys waiting to use the Porta Potti, and they were screaming at me to just shut up and show them my tits. I pretended not to hear them, but between you and me, dear diary, it was really hard not to. Today more poets had trash thrown at them on the main stage. Thank God it wasn't my turn to read.

Dear Diary, (Milwaukee)

I thought this was supposed to be like the granddaddy of alterna teen concerts, but everyone looks the same! I mean, the SAME oversized wallet chains, the same manic panic dyed hair, skinny dreads on skinny blond boys, baby Ts with cute little sayings from the seventies. God, this seventies revival thing is longer than the seventies themselves! And all these little white kids wearing oversized Dickies and Ben Davis . . . I can't help but think of all the kids I teach over in Southgate or El Monte and how they aren't allowed to wear that type of clothing 'cause it makes them look like gang members. More privileges for the white Ticketmaster class, I guess.

Dear Diary, (St. Louis)

Last week I remember thinking I was the happiest person in the whole world, in the whole universe, in all of God's creation. Could that have only been last week or was it endless light-years ago? Today, when ———— and I were waiting for the rest of the bus entourage, we talked cop shop with some state troopers. When I told them I was from L.A., they said they'd never want to work in L.A. and that the LAPD has to put up with so much shit. When I asked them what they meant, they said (and I quote), "Well, out here everyone talks American, but in L.A. you got your Orientals and your

Mexicans and you gotta talk to them and none of them speak English good, and that's stressful, and every day having all that stress and confusion, no wonder you just wanna beat the shit out of people."

Dear Diary, (Chicago)
Sorry I haven't written for a while. It's been raining. Each time a drop of rain hits me, I can swear it's a tear making up for the ones I want to cry. I don't understand it because last night I was so happy. I ate six wonderful, delicious, mouthwatering, delectable, heavenly slices of pizza but when I woke up this morning I felt horrible. Maybe it's not a good idea to eat so late at night. I had really horrible dreams and now I'm depressed. Today they told us they can't have any more poets on the main stage cuz too much trash is being thrown at them and it's damaging stage equipment. So now we are relegated to stay in the corner, the poetry corner. All the other poets are really bugging the shit out of me. The male poets do nothing but scream and scream and go on about their penises. Everyone is reading stuff about O. J., Kurt, sex, or drugs. Nobody knows what Oxnard is and my stuff isn't going over very well. I'm actually looking forward to going home. So far this summer hasn't turned out like what I thought it would be.

Dear Diary, (Columbus)
My suede mini, the patchwork one, doesn't fit anymore. Neither do my cutoffs. I shouldn't eat the pizzas anymore, but it's really the only thing I look forward to. Today, ——— from Big Belly Burritos asked if I wanted to make extra money making burritos. He said he'd pay me seven bucks under the table. So now I roll burritos three hours a day. I like hanging out with his crew. They're really the sincerest people, besides the Tibetan monks, that I've met so far on this stupid tour, and I'm really their best roller. I saw ——— from the Breeders bite into a burrito that I personally rolled and it didn't split open at all. Well, enough of this chitty-chat and writie-write. I better help ——— think of some fun things for the little alterna teens to do tomorrow.

Dear Diary, (Cincinnati)
Yesterday the producers came to my "Grunge on a Stick" booth and told me I better get rid of them cuz ——— has crashed the tour and is on a

rampage, going after anyone who is making money off her dead husband. I told them that my "Grunge on a Stick" has nothing to do with him, but rather the whole Seattle scene. What I didn't realize was that these little things have become the "hottest item" to buy at Lollapalooza and that the press has dubbed them "Shish-Cobains." I had no idea.

Oh, also yesterday all the Road Poets had an interview with MTV. I HATE talking about poetry. I mean, come on, what can you possibly say? It's like talking about sex, I'd rather just do it than talk about it. Ha, ha! No, but I never know what to say, cuz you sound either arrogant or boring or just plain show-offy. So I really didn't say much and when our segment was aired, I wasn't even mentioned. I felt really left out. Just like in Mr. ———'s English class.

Dear Diary, (?)*
Today I went skateboarding with ———. I bought me my own skateboard and then I had it signed by all the bands. He said I should pray that one of them dies of an overdose or something and then my board will be worth so much money. So anyway, we were surrounded by acres and acres of cornfields and the sun was setting and it was so nice. Until he asked, shouldn't you be at the corner reading your poetry? And then I felt guilty. But the thought of going back to the poetry corner and reading to stoned frat boys with tribal tattoos was just too depressing.

Dear Diary, (?)
Sorry I haven't written for a while. I've been depressed. We've been to so many places I've lost track of time and places. I called ——— today long distance and cried when I heard her voice. When I told her I was working making burritos, she said, "Michele, you shouldn't be rolling burritos. You're there to read your poetry." But when I told her I liked the burrito makers more than the poets, and that I liked making burritos more than reading poetry, she just said, "You're making us all look bad." Later I didn't know if she meant I make other poets look bad or other brown people (of whom I haven't seen any in a long time) look bad. Oh, and today this girl

---

* *There are no dates or locations for the following material. It was recorded on single sheets of paper, set lists, place mats, etc.*

BEGGED me for my all-access badge. I've seen her at the last three venues working at one of the feminist tables and she said, "Please, please, please, I have to meet —— from the Smashing Pumpkins!" But when I casually mentioned to her that he was married, she said, "I don't wanna meet his wife, I just wanna fuck HIM." Oh, like I should have known better.

Dear Diary, (?)

I'm taking a break from the tour. I'm sick of the poets and the poetry corner and all the male poets that scream, scream, scream. I decided to go into Ann Arbor with everyone from Big Belly Burritos. In order to get the ride I had to help break down their stand and now I still reek of onions and bleach. We had to all sit in the back of a U-Haul truck with no windows or air and I was warned that —— wakes up in his sleep and pisses on people. I didn't sleep at all, all night.

Dear Diary, (NYC)

Oh, the New York poets are the best! Man, they must write and practice a lot. They can think up poems quickly and lay down rhymes and just recite them quick. I wish I could do that. I am so jealous. It's raining and there's mud everywhere and I've lost my favorite platforms. I really just want to go home. Only one more day to go. I saw —— backstage and I hear she hands out candy in exchange for borrowing equipment. Her toenail polish is chipped. Tacky.

Dear Diary,

Well, the tour is officially over for me. What a summer! I don't want to hear or read anything in stanzas for a while. If I see one more burrito, I will throw up and if I hear that screaming intro for "Sabotage" one more time, *I'll* scream! I am writing this from the train. I decided to take a train home rather than fly. It will take three days and —— said I was crazy to take the train back to L.A., but I don't care. I wanna see the country. I wanna take my time and think about things for a while. Right now I'm eating an orange yeast roll I bought from the snack machine and it is so, so delicious. I can feel its warmth and am actually experiencing the orange zest. It's a thousand times better, a million, trillion times better than all that catered crap they served us on tour. I'm sitting across from an Amish family and they look so content and stress-free. No airs or gimmicks. I mean, what's it like to be so disciplined and humble and use craftsmanship for practical reasons? What's it like making art not just to show off and get attention? I wonder what it would be like to live on an Amish farm. Could I live on an Amish farm? I will definitely check into that for next summer. Yes, I'm gonna make next summer the best summer of my life. See ya!

PART TWO

# poetry

# Grammarotics

NICK CARBÓ

The angle of delight is best
achieved while rubbing

the pluperfect button
in tiny syllabic circles

while the glottal stop needs
firm accentual strokes

for copulative conjunction
to occur. The placement

of the preterite tense
at the entrance

of a lubricated sentence
assures the inevitable

apostrophe. However,
if the apostrophe occurs

prematurely the result
is then a dangling

modifier, also
commonly known as

a pathetic fallacy.

# Ang Tunay Na Lalaki Is Addicted to New York

NICK CARBÓ

fantasy phone sex
and he swims
the voodoo

of her voice
@ $4.99/minute,
asking her to repeat

"I am a possessed witch."
Her name is Anne
and she blows

smoke on his thighs
as he slumps himself
on his easy chair.

She gives good
similes and his penis
is as big as Brazil,

as warm as an incandescent
light bulb, as hard
as Muhammad Ali's jaw.

She tantalizes him
with fancy words like
*tristesse, ennui, juxtapose,*

*cicatrix*, and *hyperbole*.
With each savory syllable,
her tongue trochees

from the base
to the top of his penis,
spondees around the head.

# wishes for sons

LUCILLE CLIFTON


i wish them cramps.
i wish them a strange town
and the last tampon.
i wish them no 7-11.

i wish them one week early
and wearing a white skirt.
i wish them one week late.

later i wish them hot flashes
and clots like you
wouldn't believe. let the
flashes come when they
meet someone special.
let the clots come
when they want to.

let them think they have accepted
arrogance in the universe,
then bring them to gynecologists
not unlike themselves.

# Ballade for the Missing Beat

ALLISON JOSEPH

What's up with Harmony, and Yo-Yo, too?
Has anybody heard from Humpty Hump?
Kris Kross and Young MC, what did they do
to disappear from sight? Nobody plays "Jump"
or "Bust a Move"—those hits that used to bump
from boom boxes, car speakers. Don't hear
those jams no more—their jolting thump.
Where are those rapping stars of yesteryear?

X-Clan, that ultra-righteous crew
used to drop science, with beats they'd pump
in darkest pride. Jungle Brothers once were new,
and De La Soul, and why not lump
in Tribe Called Quest? What slump
has silenced Special Ed for years?
And what of Bushwick Bill, that little chump?
Where are those rapping stars of yesteryear?

And what about those rappers who
became cartoons, like Kid 'n' Play? I'm stumped
as to where they are. They're gone from view,
their lunch boxes and toys left in a dump
somewhere. Where's Chubb Rock, that plump
delightful fellow, and is Biz Markie near?
And Sister Souljah, that scowling frump?
Where are those rapping stars of yesteryear?

MC Hammer!—Once he lived like Trump.
Remember when the Geto Boys stoked fear?
Remember when the Fat Boys shook their rumps?
Where are those rapping stars of yesteryear?

# Role Models

ALLISON JOSEPH

The next time a man demands to know
who my literary foremothers are, I want
to see his jaw drop when I say, straight-

faced, Wonder Woman, the Bionic Woman,
and Supergirl. I want to see him nod politely
when I reveal my childhood's pivotal moment—

watching Lynda Carter chase crooks in a red,
white and blue bustier, fighting crime and
busting Nazis with bullet-repellent bracelets

and her golden lasso of truth. I loved how
she'd spin around, transform from mousy
military secretary into a well-endowed crusader

for justice and the common good. Even
my father commented approvingly: That woman
sure has some big lungs, he'd say, admiring

cleavage that bobbed as she pursued the baddest
of bad guys. She even piloted an invisible plane,
had a whole island of Amazonian sisters for backup.

That's very nice, my companion will say, shying away
during this reverie, leaving me alone to ponder
the Bionic Woman and Supergirl, their places in the canon

less secure, their derivation from male heroes.
Still, all three made me want to fly, and what's more feminist
than challenging who can take off, who stays bound to the ground?

# Invocation for a Future Diva

ALLISON JOSEPH


I need a diva I can believe in, someone
whose voice makes me forget whatever else
has made me angry, made me mad,

someone I can wail along with on love songs
so corny I'd be ashamed to sing the lyrics
in public, songs full of trills, vocal leaps,

catchy choruses that linger when I go
to bed, refrains on my lips when
I wake. But who's out there among

pop-star divas on the scene today—
who's got the lung power, star power,
who can stun the glitterati and paparazzi

all at once while still making music
for me, a woman singing while her
laundry spins, her dishes soak?

There's Celine, who I wish had gone down
with the ship; Mariah, who reminds me
of the slutty girl in high school whose name

got scrawled all over bathroom stalls,
regardless of whom she actually screwed;
and Whitney, who reminds me of that girl

in high school voted "most likely
to achieve something none of the rest
of us could while stabbing everyone

along the way in the back." Then
there are the minidivas, who should
be in high school, and are of little use

to me on my quest for a diva
whose voice can remake the molecules
of this world: Brandy Britney Mandy Mya

Christina—girls who wouldn't
know a stretch mark from a track mark,
who think Motown is some kind

of suburban relocation project. I need
a diva with some wear in this world,
a sob in her voice not created by studio

engineers. There are the old-school divas:
Chaka Aretha Etta Diana Tina—
but I'm longing for a new voice,

notes I haven't heard sung precisely
that way before, a new set of tics
and triumphs. I want someone

unexpected, someone who's only pretty
when the stage lights hit, a shy superstar
who will not fade from my memory

quicker than last week's last lunch.
Then it hits me: I'll have to give birth
to this new diva myself, raise her

from infancy to sing along with old
Tammi Terrell–Marvin Gaye records,
pay for her singing lessons, tap-dance

sessions, toe shoes, leotards, choreographer—
all the accoutrements that turn little girls
into sensations on sold-out cross-country tours.

I pat my stomach, knowing my womb
could bring to this earth a creature with a voice
so undeniable that I'd spend my old age

basking in reflected glory. Then I glimpse
my snoring sleeping husband, wonder when
there will be time for baby-diva making,

and I turn back over, pull up
my blankets, turn off the light,
and I go back to sleep.

# Care and Feeding of Writers

ALLISON JOSEPH

Assume that their childhoods scarred them,
so have plenty of wine on hand—red
for the bleeders, white for the overtly teary.
Expect chronicles of broken marriages
so elaborate you'll wish you'd gotten them all
on tape, all those gothic convolutions:
who threw whom down the stairs,
who lopped off a sleeping mate's ponytail.
Expect ex-lovers, ex-wives, ex-husbands,
ex-priests, red-faced bosses, blue-haired
mothers, pierced and tattooed daughters,
sons who shoot on sight, inspect later.
For each story, provide rewards:
clove cigarettes, alpaca sweaters, imported
cheeses. Make sure their beds harbor
the right pillows, blankets, comforters;
keep them warm as they stumble
up the stairs to the guest room
or to the hotel suite on floor fourteen.
Tell them the room will stop spinning,
you're sure of it. Bring them vitamins
and freshly squeezed orange juice,
but skip the eggs—too symbolic,
loaded with blatant meanings
the best writers avoid. Feed them
whole wheat pancakes with melting butter
instead, comfort food to settle the stomachs
of the almost great, the perennially jealous,
the sullen and secretive scribes who caravan
through town two or three at a time, dragging
their battered psyches and suitcases behind them.

# In Praise of the Penis

ALLISON JOSEPH

Funny little fellow,
all our slang for you
is harsh—prick, dick, cock—
hard consonants erupting
from our mouths, jutting like
the bulge on the school jock.
But usually you're quite
harmless, sleepy as a baby
and just as needy.
You're quite laughable, really—
rod, tool, yardstick—I don't care
what you call yourself,
how you glorify your shape
and/or size, you'll forever
seem to me to be some sort
of elevated inchworm,
a fleshy extraterrestrial
from late-night sci-fi—
instead of The Blob,
my marquee reads The Penis—
mobs of screaming virgins,
clad in kneesocks and angora,
run to escape a creature
who's come to life in 3-D,
threatening the town's very virtue.
Most undignified fellow,
I won't leave your care
to anyone else, won't
replace you with some toy
bought from the back of a magazine.
You fascinate me, though
I've seen your act before—

the humble slow awakenings,
firecracker finishes. Still,
I'm always glad when you
decide to let loose once more,
spilling on newly washed sheets
until you're weary, bashful, spent.

# Hell Pig

AIMEE NEZHUKUMATATHIL


To keep me from staying out late at night,
my mother warned of the *Hell Pig*. Black and full

of hot drool, eyes the color of a lung—it'd follow me
home if I stayed past my curfew. How to tell my friends

to press *Pause* in the middle of a video, say their good-byes
while I shuffled up the stairs and into my father's waiting

blue car? How to explain this to dates, whisper
why we could not finish this dance? It's not like the pig

had any special powers or could take a tiny bite
from my leg—only assurances that it was simply

scandal to be followed home. When my date and I
pull into the driveway and dim the lights, we

take care to make all the small noises that get made
in times like these even smaller: squeaks in the seats,

a slow spin of the radio dial, the silver click of my belt.
Too late. A single black hair flickers awake the ear

of the dark animal waiting for me at the end of the walk.
My fumbling of keys and various straps a wild dance

to the door—the pig grunting in tune to each hurried step, each
of his wet breaths puffing into tiny clouds, a small storm brewing.

# Swear Words

AIMEE NEZHUKUMATATHIL

Even now I laugh when I see the look on my mother's face
when I swear in Tagalog. I have no idea what these phrases
really mean, but they've been spattered on me since I was still
a fat, bawling baby—and scattered onto my head when I've toppled

juice glasses on white carpet or come home past curfew.
Sometimes even the length of my skirts or driving her through
a red light produces ones with a bit of a gasp, a wet sigh
of disapproval. Now I catch myself saying them out loud

when I knock my knee against the coffee table,
slice a bit of my knuckle with paper. When I asked her,
she told me one phrase meant "God," so of course I felt guilty.
Another is "crazy female lost piglet," which doesn't even

make sense when I think of the times I've heard her use that.
Still others, she claims, are untranslatable. But the one
I love best is *Diablo*—devil—pronounced: *Jah-blew!* She uses it
as if to tell me, "I give up! You do what you want but don't

come running to me," after I tell her I bounced a check
or messed up a romance with a boy she finally approved of.
*Diablo! Diablo!* Here comes a little red devil running past
the terra-cotta flowerpots in my mother's sunroom, tiny pitchfork

in hand. *Diablo! Diablo!* And still another from behind
the kitchen curtains, a bit damp from the day's splashes of the sink.
Today when they meet, they dance a silly jig on the countertop, knock
over the canister of flour, leave little footprints all over the place.

# the night my mother meets bruce lee

PAISLEY REKDAL

China smokes under a tree. That's how low
    mist settles in this picture, bad brush painting
where silver maids crouch like silver wolves
    wailing for a man who'll come
from the moon. There are dishes. In the restaurant
    my mother loads up red tubs
of spilled noodles, shuffles toward the one white
    customer who watches. *You know the story*
*behind that painting?* My mother doesn't.
    The man's face falls, a little florid, too
open like the jar of her mother's pastel
    peonies so enormous with want, she can't
believe these are flowers her own mother
    displays on waxed tabletops, petals arranged
in shredded pleats as if the flower were swelling
    in its own desire. She doesn't know anything,
my mother: not the fat and dirty carp in its tank,
    what the inscrutable phoenix rises out of.
*Autumn leaves are falling like rain* is a poem which never
    penetrates the bell-shaped, woolen skirt hand-
sewn thankfully *sans* poodle, *sans* glitter peony,
    rough as her nails which glisten only
when varnished with the grease of someone else's leftovers.
    *All my neighbors are barbarians and you,*
*you are a thousand miles away* is a tune
    from a distinctly different planet
where radio towers do not thrum with
    Buddy Holly, mothers never chide in strange
tongues. My mother has a smile trained
    to kindle nebula, hurl satellites into space.
No, she doesn't have the willowy thighs of any
    of the seven maids hanging in their one frame,

the bangs of a Veronica Lake.
    Now the newest busboy erupts
out of the back kitchen, Vesuvian, a smatter
    of duck fat and ash.
"I come from Hong Kong from real
    Chinese," he told my mother. Posed
with martial vigilance, scared the cook,
    cut his thumb on a knife blade. *Kung
Fooey* everyone at the restaurant
    calls him who wields his shoulders like pickaxes
and leers at the waitresses. *I hate that
    son of a bitch*, mumbles the cashier.
The busboy mugs: a film star by the fire escape.
    *What I wouldn't do to be famous*, my mother thinks.
The answer's nothing. My mother will do
    nothing to be famous. *Although my neighbors
are barbarians and you, you are a thousand
    miles away, there are always
two cups at my table* a song
    on the restaurant tape drones mysteriously.
Customers file past my mother, a prop
    in the dullest film of all time. She'll buy
a cashmere sweater in pink tonight,
    take herself to the pictures on Sunday. At sixteen,
my mother thinks it's what
    she's supposed to want. She thinks
it's going to make her happy.

# a crash of rhinos

PAISLEY REKDAL

What's your pet name? Collective noun?
What will Snookums do today? Your bedmate
pulls quarters magically from behind your ear, one
for each hour you've spent together. When he stops
there's fifty cents sliding into the sheets and his tongue
covering the pink cauliflower of your nipple. "Beautiful
defects," he whispers into your body. "Ah, Nature." Roll away,
don't care when he calls you "Thumper." By noon you'll be
nose to nose anyway, a sloth of bears, snoozing
your way into this relationship.

Ah, Nature. You could tell him its startling fact
is not its defects but its sameness. A uniformity
suggestive of some single cell prototype, our Adam/Eve
genome plucked, as scientists think, from the thread
of a lightning bolt. Darling, today you're more
than anonymous, one sexy blip among the thousand
couples grunting in each other's arms; defined by Loving,
your action. Flying geese only recognized
by the form they make in the sky.
A crash of rhinos, piece of asses. Stinkhead:
everything comes in boring droves of hogs.

This is how you got here. Mid-morning he tallies your union
in terms of snakes, tarantulas, the evolutionary needs
of common flagellates till you scorn science: its primal
urge to pair like scared cows shoved ass to ass in circles
for defense. A clutch of penises. What is love but fear?
That soft storm at your periphery, sudden hand
pushing you below surface? Thoughts, as you age or sicken,
sifted from consciousness like dusts of starlings: Love me,
little lamb. No one should die alone.

Sweetheart, all your friends are married.
Packs of teazles? Kerfs of panters? A multiplicity of spouses.
Today only two quarters protect you
from loneliness. It's out of your hands. The job
didn't pan, checks bounce, 2 A.M. is its own
worst child. This is your last magic trick.
"Kumquat," he whispers. Lover. Loved one.
And the soul begs always, *Leave me leave me*
while the body says simply, *Stay*.

# love phones

PAISLEY REKDAL

## the problem

"OK so I'm a lesbian," begins tonight's show and it's Caitlin
worried that her girlfriend now likes men
but won't come out. "Beautiful," moans the intern
as the certified sex therapist–cum–show host giggles
in the mic. They've got solid radio
format: good host/bad host. Dr. Judy's sweet while Jagger
sneers at gay men and adolescents. So

"I don't get," says the third girl this evening, "why
my boyfriend stops talking after we have sex,"
and it's Jagger's turn: "Because you're dull."
After two hours of this, it's true—everyone's
dull. Even the mother caught at the neighborhood orgy
by her 17-year-old, the boy who masturbates in the county abattoir,
the wife who wakes each day with sperm
lacing her face. It's understood

the advice is meant to be educational
for those neophytes of love, the public school sex
-ed flunkees whose already watered understanding
of sex consists solely of having gotten pregnant; Aphrodite's
least learned, most deprived, or simply dumbest
percentage of America's population. "Well Caitlin,"

purrs Judy, "What is it about your girlfriend's attraction
to men that bothers you?" *Beep.*
Jagger disconnects the line the second she stammers.
By 11:10 the usual has happened:
some earnest fan calls in to chastise him for thoughtlessness.
Just what does he do besides harass? Jagger plays up rage.

"Are you getting wood there?" he spits.
"Does this sort of thing turn you on, you pimple,
you ass. . . ." Mid-sentence the satellite

transmission's switched. The station's back
to rock format till 2 A.M. while we, insistently
disinterested, are left afloat in bed.
Up to our necks in today's dishes and work, garbage still
swaddled in sacks. The argument dangles mid-air.
We have to wait till tomorrow night
when the show returns to find life out.
For another day of America's tuned-in
radioed troubles to yet again start over.


## the intern

Because it's radio and their voices are smooth, because it's sex
they air the hosts get more fan mail than their looks deserve. Dr. Judy,
one man demurs, must be a vixen. But I know best, having
worked the late shift at the station. "Subbing,"

they call it, when the normal host goes face down
in the free tequila handed out at Promotions.
I'm the one left standing who sets the Demods
up for Go, passes Tylenol and headphones out
like Kleenex in the control room. When the call for me first
came through it wasn't unusual:
for female DJs, radio's a magnet for solitudes
who think the visual is an imposition.
By midnight, we're anyone's face.

                              "Do you pull your panties off one leg
at a time?" he'd asked. "Do you like to suck your fingers?"
"Screw you," I said and hung up. But the threat must have come off
as an imperative; every night at twelve o'clock, he calls.

"I can tell you're smart," he said after our third conversation.
"You don't want to suck my cock, do you?"

                                    Meanwhile Judy's regulars complain
about the soullessness of dating. "It's like,"
says caller number two, "I have this deep dark hole
I just can't fill." Which is, Jagger proclaims, just
what we're here to do. Night's for The Lonely Hearts: jokers
scratching bathroom stalls full
of phone numbers who find our hotline call-in stapled
next to posters of Asian girls and Danish cheerleaders
broadcasting universal help, help help
translated to show and more show. So

"Let's talk more about her deep dark hole,"
Jagger growls, and I picture stars sucked like cue balls
into crushing space pockets centimeters wide; perhaps (this
with guilt) a thirteen-year-old and her first makeshift
shortwave radio in a blacked-out park,
letting the world's silky tongues roll over her.
For better or for worse, settling on us. And always: Let's talk
more about this hole, this cavity of yours eaten out
by increasing addictions to toll-free numbers; trash's sweet,
singular anxieties. . . .

                                    "I bet you're married," the Pervert said last night.
Tricked into intimacy, I'd forgotten myself and answered, "No."
"I knew it," he replied. "You just don't sound
like you'd listen to that kind of garbage."

I'm starting to think of it like advice.

## dr. judy

Famous lie: "I got into radio
Because it's not TV." When such desolate

wave lengths measure up basically the same.
Space fascinates us.
Where we find it we tend to add

and add what we cannot see, as when
the atom is revealed to be a truck-sized sack
with a few peanuts rolling in it
and we counter with cushions of charge

stuffed within, nearly undetectable by microscope or laser,
because the truth that at points the hand
is indistinguishable from the table due to
*nothing* terrifies. It's *nothing*

that connects us here in space just as *nothing*
is the key to Caitlin's lover's changed desire,
the space in and out between them, electric
hips pushed against each other
by the kitchen sink. *What is still
uncharted land, the soul?*

we've asked. No, space.
And sent men into it, monkeys; even
a woman or two has arrived back from that crushing
blue-black with bowls
of sterile dirt, the frozen crust hurled off stars
eons ago. We're amazing

ourselves more than this eternal flotsam can,
which is the soul of space
we tell ourselves, the greatest moral that exists
recast in paperweights,
health drinks, easy-to-get-in shoes.

Tang and Velcro are what we've communally gained
from the moon, I've often said.

We're a culture that values
T-shirts, pelts, evidence
of the exotic. "Any response means hope tonight,"
I tell my audience. Take scalps,

lovers. "What's wrong?" *Oh
nothing nothing nothing!* But all the peanuts
rattling in their sack tell me: It's space
between us and the world, hands
dangling through chairs and vice versa,
for the uncertainty of blood pushed mightily
through the yam-sized heart and all we've got
to show for discontent

are postcards: the husband's
nightie. The scarf of leather studs
your mother wears to our reunion. And worse:
this man who takes my daughter in the bathroom
like a drug when I'm not home.

"Just talk to me," says our intern tonight to the hotline phone while somewhere over Minsk
a satellite broadcasts every language on the Earth
including whale songs, weakly.
Our safety catch in terse hellos.

Our greetings to the universe.

# Natasha in a Mellow Mood

TIM SEIBLES

*(apologies to Bullwinkle and Rocky)*


Boris, dahlink, look
at my legs, long
as a lonely evening in Leningrad,
how they open the air
when I walk, the way moonlight
opens the dark. Boris, my hair
is so black with espionage,
so cool and quiet with all those secrets
so well kept—those secret plans
you've nearly kissed
into my ears. Who gives a proletarian
**damn** about Bullwinkle and that
flying squirrel and that idiot
who draws us? America
is a virgin, the cartoonist who leaves me
less than a Barbie doll under
this dress, who draws me
with no smell—**he** is a virgin.
The children who watch us
every Saturday mornink
are virgins. Boris, my sweet waterbug, I
don't want to be a virgin anymore.
Look into my eyes, heavy
with the absence of laughter
and the presence of vodka. Listen
to my Russian lips muss up
these blonde syllables of English:
**Iwantchu.** Last night
I dreamed you spelled your
code name on my shoulder
with the waxed sprigs of your

moustache. I had just come
out of the bath. My skin was still
damp, my hair poured like ink
as I pulled the comb through it. Then
I heard you whisper, felt you take
my hand—Oh, Boris, Boris
Badenov, I want your mischief-
riddled eyes to invent
my whole body, all the silken
slopes of flesh forgotten
by the blind cartoonist. I want
to be scribbled all over you
in shapes no pencil would dare. Dahlink,
why don't we take off
that funny little hat. Though
you are hardly tall
as my thighs, I want your pointy
shoes beside my bed, your
coat flung and fallen
like a double-agent
on my floor.

# Boris by Candlelight

TIM SEIBLES

Natasha, first this—
then what? I'll be looking
into the shadows and, instead
of that buck-toothed squirrel, I'll see
your body drawn like an ivory blade
slicing the dark. Then what good
will I be to Fearless Leader?
All of Moscow will become your
slow walk, as though the entire city
swam with your slim thighs
shortening the streets.

Natasha, we are supposed to be
comrades in the struggle—we are
supposed to be taking the world
back from America. We should be nabbing
Rocky and giving him some convincing
bonks on the head. But don't think
I haven't noticed your blouse
ripe as midnight when you pass by
at headquarters, and that sleepy
invitation in your glance when
we've been spying too long
in the White House basement,
squinting into that small
circle of light.

Once I saw the wind turn around
in your raven hair and thought
of your dress as a full sail and
myself, a small island upon which you
might be shipwrecked for an evening.

Do you really think that when I
close my eyes it's Bullwinkle
that haunts the dim hall inside me?
But, dahlink, we are supposed to be
dreaming of a more perfect State.

You must understand, Natasha,
in every frame of this life
we invent ourselves and the air.
The cartoonist is just a sad rumor,
like the distance you see between us.
These lines that shape our bodies,
that separate us and break up the world—
they're there because you think
they're there. You have always been
a part of me, Natasha. I have
already sketched you a million times
with my soul's invisible ink.
I love you as much as I live
for Russia. But these capitalists,
baby, they will snatch even the broken moon
if we look away and let them.

# cartoons and a graphic story

# A Selection of Cartoons

CHARLES JOHNSON

"I'm wearing a corsage so you'll know me."

"It's life as I see it."

"All your racial problems will soon end . . ."

"First you must lower your psychological defenses."

"I sure hope your aim is better when the revolution comes!"

" . . . Rufus turned on the white racists who breathed hotly down his back: he turned defiantly upon them, snatching the noose away from the Ku Klux Klansman and raised his clenched fist, shouting 'Black power, Black power' . . ."

"This adaptation of *Crime and Punishment* is close, Baxter, but if we change Raskolnikov to a cross-dressing, black environmentalist—I see Dennis Rodman in the role—your name will be in that envelope at Oscar time."

"Hmm, *Thirty-six Ways to Lynch Negroes.* I guess it's okay . . ."

"Gee, I'll bet you're glad to be out of the ghetto."

"Didn't I ask you not to bring your work home at night?"

"Once over that line, Whitey, consider yourself to be in the 'New Republic of Africa.'"

"Believe me, Richard, I've been in publishing for thirty years, and I can assure you a book about Black anger will simply never sell . . ."

"Oh, maybe I should have told you not to mention Spike Lee or Toni Morrison."

"Whatever you do, son, try not to let anyone know our family has only been white for 100 years."

"That's as close as this university gets to multiculturalism."

"According to this news bulletin, a new nuclear power must be acknowledged—in Harlem."

"All right, you *can* fast longer than me."

"As your mother, I knew what was best for you in my last life, Herman, and I still know . . ."

"Now what makes you think that no one gives you any respect?"

"You'll be easy on the black power, won't you, Freddie?"

"All I know is that too much one-pointedness can make you really tired."

"These author photos can be deceptive."

"OK, this week we're discussing Charles Johnson's *Dreamer*. Do you all have your dictionaries ready?"

**Draining Like a Dead Chicken**

ERIKA LOPEZ

# DRAINING LIKE A DEAD CHICKEN

A little tampon. ⎯⎯⎯ ▭
I AM ANGRY AT TAMPONS +
I DON'T WEAR THEM ANYMORE.
IT'S NOT only THAT I CAN'T
AFFORD THEM, BUT that
~~I~~ wouLDN'T wear them
EVEN if I could. I'M
a gainst paying close
To FIVE BUCKS FOR A BOX
of what is basically
COMPRESSED Toilet paper.

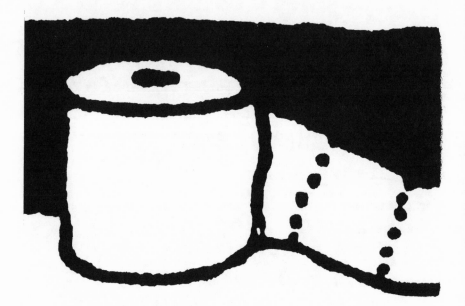

These corporate guys have REALLY GOT BLEEDING WOMEN BY THE OVARIES./ BLEEDING WOMEN IN WHITE STRETCH PANTS BY THE OVARIES: "I FEEL CONFIDENT! AND YES, I'M WILLING TO DO CARTWHEELS IN PUBLIC!"

I was convinced by a braless,
EARTH-LOVING PRINTMAKER
WHO LIVED ALONE w/ her CAT,
TO USE A SMALL SEA SPONGE.
THE KIND THEY SOLD in health
FOOD STORES in a SMALL FAKE
VELVET POUCH.

Then, while I was at THE HEALTH food STORE, I ALSO bought SOME PATCHOULI FOR MY UNBLEEDING PREMENSTRUAL WRISTS.

THEN. / THEN W/ MY HANDS
LOOKING LIKE ARTHRITIC
YAMS, I BUMPED INTO A
BOOK ABOUT WOMYN-
STUFF. IT WAS POLITELY
PRINTED IN SOY INK ON
UNBLEACHED PAPER.
IT WAS *called*:


HYGEIA/A WOMAN'S HERBAL.

It was written in the 70s, AND I COULD hear JOAN BAEZ's song, "Diamonds and Rust" as I turned the FIRST PAGE...

"On The Rag" and other menstrual rituals -- for you, fertile SISTER

THAT's what the FIRST CHAPTER WAS CALLED. + BEING THE FERTILE SISTER THAT I WAS, I READ ON...

(I shall paraphrase)

"DO NOT BE ASHAMED OF YOUR BLOOD, OH SISTER.

I LOVE YOU, VAGINAL BLOOD. AND I AM NOT ASHAMED OF YOU.

DO NOT HIDE YOUR
SOILED napkins IN THE
DARK TRASH.
TAKE your PROUD
BLOOD TO THE AIR,
THE SUN ☼ , THE
EARTH 🌍

*Let* GO OF THE EGG, AND SAY ( GOOD-BYE, EGG )

And THE PAIN WILL BE EASIER. / DO NOT BE ashamed of bleeding. PROCLAIM YOUR BLEEDING! YOUR FERTILENESS! ~ LET The WORLD KNOW / AND BE PROUD! GET in touch w/ YOUR MENSTRUAL CONSCIOUSNESS.

Squat over your HOUSEPLANTS
THAT NEED minerals. AND DO
NOT PLUG YOURSELF UP W/WHITE
PATERNAL PLUGS. BLEED

# FREELY

--- AND MAKE YOUR OWN MENSTRUAL PAD. MAKE IT HUGE. / MAKE IT PROUD. A PROUD menstrual PAD, BECAUSE There Is an art to BLEEDING. (RINSE! RECYCLE! DO NOT SUPPORT A HUGE POLLUTING INDUSTRY!)

Maybe choose a purple FLANNEL To REST NEXT to your EARTHLY VAGINA.... AND applique a gold MANDALA on the front.... WHO SAID THAT EVERYTHING Must BE WHITE LIKE THOSE HERMETICALLY SEALED TAMPONS + WEDDING DRESSES?

MOCKS YOU
FOR LIVING,
EXISTING
+
SECRETING."

THAT WAS IT. THAT WAS ALL
I NEEDED TO READ. / I PUT
THE BOOK DOWN + WALKED
AROUND MY APARTMENT
CARRYING A SPIDER PLANT
BETWEEN MY LEGS, AND
SINGING MADE UP SONGS
ABOUT GERMAINE GREER
TO CLASSICAL MUSIC WRItten
BY EXTREMELY DEAD MEN.

MY CAT FREAKED OUT
ᔕᔕᔑᔑᔓᔓᔓ
AND threatened to
leave me forever if
I didn't quit it. /
But I WAS SO EXHAUSTED
BY MY IRON DEFICIENCY,
I DIDN'T HAVE THE
STRENGTH TO TALK her
out of it. / SHE WAS
WALKING out THE DOOR
+ ALL I COULD SCREAM
BEFORE PASSING OUT ON
THE FLOOR WAS:

AND a FEW DAYs LATER,
AFTER I WAS RELEASED
FROM the HOSPITAL, I
DECIDED TO give MY
SPONGES a WHIRL.

I was PROUD AS I RINSED
them in PUBLIC SINKS,
Jamming my FOOT against
the BATHROOM DOOR. /
I FELT SUPERIOR. /
SUPERIOR LIKE A SUPERIOR
PERSON, IN BEING CONNECTED
To MY Blood / my eggs.

ME          EGG

I SAID: "FAREWELL, MY LITTLE
EGGS, FAREWELL" AS I SET
MY BLOOD FREE, DOWN THE
DRAIN. / LIKE A SAD
BIRD-MOTHER OR SOMETHING.

I WALKED BACK INTO THE
DENNY'S DINING ROOMS
FEELING CONNECTED, IF NOT
WAITED ON, AND I WAS
AT A FEMALE kind of
Peace...

But the SPONGES DETERIORATED, and the ROMANCE FADED w/ RED FAMILIARITY./PAST DUE therapy bills STARTED TAKING PRECEDENCE, AND I still HAD NO MONEY w/all the TAMPON BOYCOTT CASH I SAVED.

# PART FOUR

# nonfiction

# White Men Can't Drum

SHERMAN ALEXIE

Last year on the local television news, I watched a short feature on a meeting of the Confused White Men chapter in Spokane, Washington. They were all wearing war bonnets and beating drums, more or less. A few of the drums looked as if they might have come from Kmart, and one or two men just beat their chests.

"It's not just the drum," said the leader of the group. "It's the idea of a drum."

I was amazed at the lack of rhythm and laughed, even though I knew I supported a stereotype. But it's true: White men can't drum. They fail to understand that a drum is more than heartbeat. Sometimes it is the sound of thunder, and many times it just means some Indians want to dance.

As a Native American, I find it ironic that even the most ordinary moments of our lives take on ceremonial importance when adopted by the Men's Movement. Since Native American men have become role models for the Men's Movement, I find it vital to explain more fully some of our traditions to avoid any further misinterpretation by white men.

Peyote is not just an excuse to get high.

A Vision Quest cannot be completed in a convention room rented for that purpose.

Native Americans can be lousy fathers and sons, too.

A warrior does not necessarily have to scream to release the animal that is supposed to reside inside every man. A warrior does not necessarily have an animal inside him at all. If there happens to be an animal, it can be a parakeet or a mouse just as easily as it can be a bear or a wolf.

When a white man adopts an animal, he often chooses the largest animal possible. Whether this is because of possible phallic connotations or a kind of spiritual steroid abuse is debatable.

I imagine a friend of mine, John, who is white, telling me that his spirit animal is the Tyrannosaurus rex.

"But John," I would reply gently, "those things are all dead."

As a "successful" Native American writer, I have been asked to lecture at various men's gatherings. The pay would have been good—just a little more reparation, I figured—but I turned down the offers because I couldn't have kept a straight face.

The various topics I have been asked to address include "Native Spirituality and Animal Sexuality," "Finding the Inner Child," and "Finding the Lost Father." I figure the next step would be a meeting on "Finding the Inner Hunter When Shopping at the Local Supermarket."

Much of the Men's Movement focuses on finding things that are lost. I fail to understand how Native American traditions can help in that search, especially considering how much we have lost ourselves.

The average life expectancy of a Native American male is about 50 years—middle age for a white man—and that highlights one of the most disturbing aspects of the entire Men's Movement. It blindly pursues Native solutions to European problems but completely neglects to provide European solutions to Native problems.

Despite the fact that the drum still holds spiritual significance, there is not one Indian man alive who has figured out how to cook or eat a drum.

As Adrian C. Louis, Paiute poet, writes, "We all have to go back with pain in our fat hearts to the place we grew up to grow out of." In their efforts to find their inner child, lost father, or car keys, white males need to go way back. In fact, they need to travel back to the moment when Christopher Columbus landed in America, fell to his knees on the sand and said, "But my mother never loved me."

That is where the real discovery begins.

Still, I have to love the idea of so many white men searching for answers from the same Native traditions that were considered heathen and savage for so long. Perhaps they are popular among white men precisely because they are heathen and savage.

After all, these are the same men who look as if they mean to kill each other over Little League baseball games.

I imagine the possibilities for some good Indian humor and sadness mixed all together.

I imagine that Lester FallsApart, a full-blood Spokane, made a small fortune when he gathered glass fragments from shattered reservation-car-wreck windshields and sold them to the New Age store as healing crystals.

I imagine that six white men traveled to a powwow and proceeded to set up shop and drum for the Indian dancers, who were stunned and surprised by how much those white men sounded like clumsy opera singers.

I imagine that white men turn to an old Indian man for answers. I imagine Dustin Hoffman. I imagine Kevin Costner. I imagine Daniel Day-Lewis. I imagine Robert Bly. Oh, these men who do all of the acting and none of the reacting.

My friend John and I were sitting in the sweat lodge. No. We were actually sitting in the sauna in the YMCA when he turned to me.

"Sherman," he said, "considering the chemicals, the stuff we eat, the stuff that hangs in the air, I think the sweat lodge has come to be a purifying ceremony, you know? White men need that, to use an Indian thing to get rid of all the pollution in our bodies. Sort of a spiritual enema."

"That's a lot of bull," I replied savagely.

"What do you mean?"

"I mean that the sweat lodge is a church, not a free clinic."

The Men's Movement seems designed to appropriate and mutate so many aspects of Native traditions. I worry about the possibilities: Men's Movement chain stores specializing in portable sweat lodges; the "Indians 'R' Us" commodification of ritual and artifact; white men who continue to show up at powwows in full regalia and dance.

Don't get me wrong. Everyone at a powwow can dance. They all get their chance. Indians have round dances, corn dances, owl dances, intertribal dances, interracial dances, females dances, and yes, even male dances. We all have our places within those dances.

I mean, honestly, no one wants to waltz to a jitterbug song, right?

Perhaps these white men should learn to dance within their own circles before they so rudely jump into other circles. Perhaps white men need to learn more about patience before they can learn what it means to be a man, Indian or otherwise.

Believe me, Arthur Murray was not a Native American.

Last week my friend John called me up on the telephone. Late at night.

"Sherman," he said, "I'm afraid. I don't know what it means to be a man. Tell me your secrets. Tell me how to be a warrior."

"Well, John," I said, "a warrior did much more than fight, you know? Warriors fed their families and washed the dishes. Warriors went on Vision Quests and listened to their wives when they went on Vision Quests, too. Warriors picked up their dirty clothes and tried not to watch football games all weekend."

"Really?"

"Really," I said. "Now go back to sleep."

I hung up the phone and turned on the television because I knew it would be a long time before sleep came back to me. I flipped through channels rapidly. There was *F Troop* on one channel, *Dances with Wolves* on another, and they were selling authentic New Mexico Indian jewelry on the shopping channel.

What does it mean to be a man? What does it mean to be Indian? What does it mean to be an Indian man? I press the mute button on the remote control so that everyone can hear the answer.

# Daddy Dearest

SANDRA TSING LOH

I insist that this be the last column about my father. OK, maybe I've never actually written a whole column about him before, but I don't want this to become a habit. Understand that for years anecdotes about my father—what I thought were throwaways—were the only things anyone would remember about me. There I'd stand, one hip jutted out, bangs moussed up impressively, in my black turtleneck and beret, waving a wineglass and arguing heatedly about the potential impact of technology on performance art. I realize now that . . . well, no one cared. They wanted funny stories about my Chinese father.

Recently I ran into Paul, an experimental video maker I'd known—almost intimately—in the mid-eighties. We convened at our host's cheese platter.

"I've been wondering for years . . . ," he murmured, resting a hand lightly on my arm.

"Yes?" I breathed.

All at once a flame leapt into his eyes, his face contorting with glee. "How's your dad? Does he still wear his underwear backward and do the Chinese snake dance on Pacific Coast Highway?"

I closed my eyes in pain. No. Of course not. Well, yes.

First let us take a step backward. Forget *my* dad. Immigrant parents in general tend toward eccentricity, don't they? They arrive from the old country; then suddenly they have VCRs and Cuisinarts, their children are growing up to be monsters, and, worse, the local Ralph's stops carrying pig knuckles.

Nationality doesn't matter. My friend Fred's parents, who emigrated from France, have bathroom counters overflowing in dental floss. (They can't bear to part with anything that's been used only once.) And several years ago when Fred's cousin returned from a summer trip in London, he was greeted at the Greyhound bus station by the sight of Fred's mother waving an enormous British flag as she cried out, "Halloo! Halloo!"

Is my father really that much odder than the rest of his ilk? For the record, he does *not* wear his underwear backward. Only his sweaters. The idea is, when the elbows wear through, you just turn them around and keep going. And yes, he did perform the Chinese snake dance for us kids, naked, armed only with a fluttering beach towel as he leapt and twirled, imparting his ancient Chinese folk song with a mournful howl. (He wasn't on the PCH at the time, but what laws—physical or federal—may have been broken, I can't say.)

Still, Paul wasn't completely off the mark about the Pacific Coast Highway—Dad's lived in Malibu for some thirty years now, threatening to cause property values to tumble along with him. Once a neighbor called the police to complain that my father was hanging out his old, holey underpants to dry, Shanghai-style, on clotheslines strung out in front of the garage. Excited, my father took the moral high road: "You know what disgusts me? Their Mercedes—that symbol of American materialism! They park it on their driveway every single day!"

The complaint calls stopped, but questions remain: Does my father, a retired aerospace engineer with science degrees from Stanford, Purdue, and Cal Tech, *have* to wear holey old underpants? Is this a person who can afford, say, *new* underpants? And a Maytag dryer perhaps? Why, yes, would have to be my answer.

As with many other Hughes engineers circa 1963, my father bought his Malibu home for the then impressive price of $47,000. By now, of course, the mortgage has long since been paid off, and the property—laundry lines notwithstanding—has shot up in value. Further, my father is one of those furtive older people who have untold stocks, bonds, mutual funds, IRAs, and whatever else that they continually shift from one account to the next, even as they complain loudly about how a loaf of bread today can set you back $1.79. I have seen stacks and stacks of bank statements stuck into drawers, all rubber-banded together and wrapped tightly in little plastic Lady Lee sandwich bags.

I don't want to give the impression that my father is rolling in cash. After all, lawsuits are regularly hurled at him by his second (ex) wife—the hot-headed Chinese one he brought over from the mainland after a brisk, eerily cheerful exchange of letters and photos. Once here, Liu made it clear that her big ambition was to break in to Hollywood. (As she spoke no English, Chinese folk singing was her "hook.") So maybe Liu did have unreasonable expectations of America. There was bound to be friction. On the other hand, I did side with her on the transportation matter. . . .

For as long as I can remember, my father has, uh, hitchhiked in and out of Malibu. (I ask you: When will it end? When will it end?) Yes, he owns a car (he even bought me one—a Hyundai; he had to shelter income). But driving is so wasteful. The RTD is terrific, but only runs about once an hour. Besides, he meets such nice people.

I have never actually seen him—at the corner of Wilshire and Fourth Street, let's say, clutching his Lucky grocery bag of scientific papers (why spend money on a briefcase?)—and not picked him up. That would be a little too "how sharp the serpent's tooth." But I have been tempted to press my foot against the gas and speed forward toward the Pacific, happy and free, like people whose seventy-year-old dads aren't still copping rides from the public.

"So I'm standing at the corner of Wilshire and Ocean, trying to flag a ride," he tells me grandly last week. (To him, all cars are potential cabs.) "It's a good spot, very visible."

"Uh-huh," I say.

"And a beautiful, elegant lady in a Mercedes picks me up." (Mercedes are not quite so disgusting when they're giving him rides.) "And she looks familiar to me, very familiar."

I brace myself.

"She knows a lot about Bill and Hillary," my father rushes on. (Almost as much as he does, being his unspoken implication.) "She met them at the White House. We had a nice conversation about them. And then I say, 'I don't know much about the movies—but I know you! Can I get your autograph?' And she writes it for me, look."

To Mr. Loh,
　It was a pleasure to have you in my car.
　Love,
　Anjelica Huston
　xxx

"Do you know her?" my father asks, beaming. "A very nice lady. She was very knowledgeable about Chinese opera and film," he chats airily. "Her father was the film director John Huston," he drops, in case I don't know this. Unlike Ms. Huston, I didn't go into my father's line of work, and this has always been a bit of a disappointment for him.

Then again, while Anjelica Huston was a good ride, she was not a dream ride. "She had another friend to drop off in Beverly Hills," he says, leaning in confidingly, looking a bit sad, "which took me a little out of my way. It would have been quicker for me to hop on the crosstown bus—I had a transfer—but by then . . ." He lowers his voice, an expert in such delicate matters of decorum, "I thought getting out might be a bit rude."

# We Do Not Live Here, We Are Only Visitors

PAISLEY REKDAL

In Taipei one of the first things I notice are the white cotton masks strapped to the faces of the women. Men wear them, too, but the number of women wearing these makeshift face-filters exceeds the number of men, and gives Taipei the look of being run by a skinny, anonymous band of surgeons.

After two days my mother, who notices this as well, wants to buy a mask for herself. I argue against it more vehemently than the situation requires, saying that we will only be in Taipei twelve days; whatever damage meant to be done to our lungs in that time will not magically be eliminated by a piece of cotton with two rubber bands. But my mother insists. Near the markets where they sell the masks, she spends minutes haggling with the merchant for a better price than she believes she is being offered. I lounge and snort, tug her away when the merchant's gesticulations become too frenzied to be understood.

In restaurants we argue halfheartedly about the necessity of the masks until we reach a compromise. Now she walks around clutching an old scarf to her face and breathing shallowly. Soon we notice older Chinese women doing the same. Only the young women seem to have adopted the ear-band model. With my mother's wiry skunk hair and still-unlined almond eyes peeking over the tips of her scarf, she has the perfect outfit for traveling. Her brown scarf allows her to blend in with the crowds of older Chinese women in the markets and on the street while always covering her mouth, muffling the fact that she can't speak Chinese.

At night in Taipei after my mother dozes off in front of the hotel television, I think about Mark in Seattle, how we argue in bed together about whether we should marry. Mark had almost proposed twice but thought better of it, he said, when he recalled how easily I became seasick. Mark is an Englishman from Kent who works as a navigator for certain shipping companies. We met in Ireland, where I lived for a year; he followed me home when I returned to Seattle. Mark had half the year off from work and decided, in his typically spontaneous fashion, to buy a plane ticket to the States the morning he drove me to the airport. Within two weeks of my return he was sharing my room in the house I rented with friends.

Mark has hired himself out as a sailing instructor now and spends the better part of every weekend teaching his latest student the rudiments of tacking. I can't spend more than a few minutes on a boat without being overcome by nausea. Besides the fact of my seasickness, however, I have found other, more pressing reasons to be hesitant about marriage, such as our inability to agree on anything. Still, marriage seems like the next logical step we need to take in our relationship, and for a while we have pursued the subject relentlessly. But whatever reasons we could invent for ourselves to believe marriage is the right answer, neither of us makes a move to propose. We have stopped referring to marriage at all; my nausea has become a symbol of our stasis. "I'm going sailing," Mark will say, looking meaningfully at me. "Do you want to come?" And I, bilious at the sight of a dock, shake my head.

In the past weeks we have argued so much that we have stopped conversing almost altogether, replacing normal dialogue with sexual banter, teasing each other about our accents. "Zee-bra," I say. "Zeh-bra," Mark answers. Tonight in Taipei in front of the flickering television, I think about his pink hands. The way his face always appears chapped in the sunset. I won't admit it to him, but I love his accent. The first time my maternal grandmother, Po Po, met him was at her birthday celebration at my parents' house in Seattle. "I can't understand a thing he says," she announced loudly after he'd greeted her.

In bed sometimes he asks me to recite the few Chinese phrases I know. *"Kai nooey,"* I say, stroking his chin. *"Gung hay fat choi. Shie shei. Soo jiep."* But his favorite is the insult: the epithet Po Po called my father before my parents married.

*"Loh fan,"* I murmur, kissing him. "Old savage. *Loh fan.*"

In Taipei my mother asks about Mark. At first she didn't approve of my sleeping with him out of wedlock and, on their first meetings, had to mask her dislike of him on account of this with excessive politeness. My mother's politeness is terrifying. I've learned about this from ex-boyfriends who insist my mother is the most intimidating woman they have ever met; a single dinner once reduced a man named Tim to sweats and stutters. But when I confront her about this on a tour of the city, she acts playfully bemused.

"They're afraid of me?" She laughs. "I'm so nice."

"It's the niceness that's killing them. They think you're really pointing out their flaws."

"If their flaws are so obvious then I don't have to point them out, do I?" she asks. "It must be cultural. Politeness like that is very Chinese."

My mother has softened toward Mark since she suspects the relationship won't last. She gathers this from the number of times Mark and I fight, the days I've called her up, still yelling my side of the argument because Mark has stormed out of the house and stranded me with my anger. Any time we spend alone together, my mother feels free to question me so intimately that I have begun to suspect her concern really fronts some prurient desire to live through me vicariously. "Oh, you're just in this for the sex," she'll say, and then accuse me of innocence, of becoming steeped in the romantic tripe that has similarly ruined her generation of friends' marriages. To defend myself I try to dismantle my image as naïf as quickly and finally as possible by confessing the most embarrassing, cruel details of our couple-hood; things I know I shouldn't tell her even as I reveal them, because if the relationship is going to lead to anything, some amount of privacy and trust has to be preserved. She knows this.

"You don't understand," I say.

"Oh, I do. You're fickle," she replies, and then demands to hear, yet again, how Mark drunkenly begged me to propose to him on New Year's and then, laughing, told me no. She tells me my boy-craziness is only exceeded by my gullibility when I tell her about the time I got so stoned I ended up in a corner and wouldn't leave until Mark, drunk himself, wrestled me out of my clothes and then left me there, naked. I embarrass myself, admitting these details. But I realize how proud my lack of loyalty to Mark makes me, how these secret transgressions increase my sense of independence. The more I tell my mother, the further apart I feel from him. "She wants to know," I tell myself. I feel like I can punish him.

By the seventh month of living with Mark, it was as if my mother had wormed her way into my skin, lodging there like a tick. Even now when Mark touches me after I spend a day alone with my mother, I become distant. I imagine she is there, bobbing above us along the ceiling. The next day the phone rings and I know it is her. I can hear her even before I pick up the receiver, her private ticking, how she is prepared to translate everything.

No one associates my mother and me with each other. To shopkeepers and hotel bellhops in Taipei we are two women traveling together, one white and one Chinese. Only when I address her as "Mom" within earshot of a Taiwanese is our situation made clear. "Your daughter?" he or she will stammer at this revelation, then I am scrutinized. I sometimes wonder what people make of our obvious age discrepancy, how they would explain the older Chinese woman paying for the restaurant and hotel bills and clothes, what kind of relationship they could possibly expect between us. On the streets young women hold hands, cuddle, rest their heads on each other's shoulders. They walk arm in arm, like nineteenth-century couples, helping each other over puddles and curbs. My mother and I, when we travel, often walk like that together in public, where at home we would never think of doing it. In Taipei my mother takes my elbow at every corner (for my safety, not hers; she's fearless in traffic), runs her hand along my back in restaurants or while waiting in long lines. Occasionally people look.

I don't blame the shopkeepers and bellhops for not immediately understanding our relationship. My mother and I really don't look alike, though during the trip I begin to insist that we do. On Christmas Eve, I stand beside her facing the hotel mirror as we make up our faces and say, "I have your nose."

"You do not have my nose," she replies, looking at me out of the corner of her eye.

"I do. Look, there's your nose."

"You don't look a thing like me."

"Mark says we have the same smile," I say, grinning widely to show her.

At this she snorts. "I don't think Mark sees you the way I see you."

"No, he sees me better. He's not as biased. Look," I say, and tilt my face so that its roundness becomes more apparent. "The same face."

"You look more like your father," she says then, ending the discussion. I can't argue with this. I do look more like my father— brown hair, narrow nose, even a chin that gently recedes in the same manner, though I do not have his light blue eyes and his broad shoulders. Still, I am taller than my mother, and thinner. Tonight, next to my mother in the mirror, I am struck by a sudden wave of vanity. I imagine that my face, next to hers, seems to glow. I pretend that my skin looks taut, my cheekbones sculpted. For those few imagined minutes my features are no longer a mark of oddity or Western exoticism, but of beauty. In this mirror I look more beautiful than my mother. And I feel strangely distant, cut off from her as if she were covered by a veil.

On the street people stare at me, but not because I am beautiful. Taipei is not populated with hordes of white Westerners, like Tokyo or Hong Kong. Here I am scrutinized, though politely, by passersby. They do not, I believe, ever recognize that I am half Chinese. They do not realize that my mother and I know each other. I walk quickly while my mother tends to shuffle; ten minutes into any walk my mother ends up six feet or more behind me. No one, unless they suspect that she is my handservant (as my mother jokes), would place the Chinese matron with the white girl.

Watching my mother in shopwindows, I see her round smooth face with the curls of permed hair, the thicker lips and wide nose. I remember the childhood friend who visited my home and met her for the first time. "What is your mother?" he had asked in private afterward. He did not, I notice, ask the same question about me.

Appearance is the deciding factor of one's ethnicity, I understand; how I look to the majority of people determines how I should behave and what I should accept to be my primary culture. This is not simply a reaction white America has to race. If for the past several years I have become a part of white America it is because it has embraced me so fully, because it is everywhere, because it is comfortable to disappear into, and because the Chinese would not recognize me on sight. Any struggle to assert myself as more than what I seem to be is exhausting. A choice, I realized, either could be made by me or asserted for me. Alone in the bathroom, I plucked my thick Asian eyebrows down to niggling scrubs and watched my brown eyes grow wide in my face, less hooded, more Italian-looking. Only when I am shown photos of myself and see the new frozen images of me, the overplucked brows and insincere half-smile slapped onto my face, do I become disturbed. Only when I say, "I'm sure I don't look like that," and my friends agree—"No, you don't look like that in real life, you look very different"—

does it occur to me what façade I am staring at. What digs at me so painfully when I see myself.

We are not visiting relatives in this country. We are visiting over the Christmas holidays, we tell strangers who ask, and we know no one in all of Taipei.

In shops my mother pretends she understands the salespeople when they speak to her. But even if she knew as much Mandarin as Cantonese, there is no way she could translate a sentence spoken by a Taiwanese six-year-old, let alone the murderously fast speech of an adult.

In Sogo Department Store, a young saleswoman with spidery eyebrows approaches my mother by a rack of sweaters. The girl wears a black tunic over a white shirt and black stockings. She barely lifts her feet when she walks: what my mother calls "the Chinese shuffle." She notices my mother fingering the material of a red sweater and immediately pounces on the garment's tag, lecturing, I suppose, on its exact blend and weave. I am guessing she tells my mother about how cool it will be for summer. My mother nods and grunts, lets escape a few of the guttural "Ahs" that have begun to punctuate her speech in Taiwan. Suddenly, I realize where she has picked this up; behind me two women converse about the merits of a handbag, and when one speaks, the other replies by fiercely grunting "Ah." My mother is mimicking her.

"Mom," I say, pointing to my watch. The salesgirl turns to me and narrows her eyes. She looks from my mother to me, the sweater dangling from her fingers. She continues speaking to my mother in Chinese though it is obvious that my mother does not know what she is talking about and that the salesgirl, like the signature seal-makers and waitresses before her, is merely babbling to herself. The salesgirl stops and clears her throat. I come forward to stand by my mother's side.

"Where are you from?" she asks in English.

"Washington. Seattle," my mother replies. She looks at me.

"Your daughter?" the salesgirl manages to get out. "She is very . . . tall." Then she walks away.

"Mom," I say later, at a restaurant for lunch, "you shouldn't do that."

"It's rude to tell her I speak English."

"It's rude to let her go on like that."

"I can understand some things she says," my mother says defensively.

But she doesn't really. I can tell by her blank expression and fierce, repetitive "Ahs" during these moments that she's simply trying to cover up.

"She wasn't speaking Cantonese."

"I meant I understood her gestures."

We sit at the dim sum restaurant in silence. My mother has successfully ordered in Chinese, but when the dishes come they are the same dishes we eat in Seattle with Po Po and the same ones we ate yesterday and the day before. I suddenly realize that my mother has been ordering only the foods whose names she knows. On the plane she had declared that she would eat dog before we left, but I can see, with a mixture of disappointment and relief, that this is a prophecy that will not come true. My mother doesn't know the word "dog" in Chinese. Tonight we pick at our food while planning our next day together and I tell her, again, how much I love oyster hash.

When Mark asks about my family, he is relieved to learn that not only I, but my mother and my mother's mother, were all born in Washington State. "Oh," he says. "That's different."

The history of my family is complicated and vaguely dangerous, as my Aunt Opal insinuates through long looks and abrupt silences at the dinner table. There is something about a tong war, sudden deaths, a disease that couldn't be cured by anything but a special herb that grows only in Canton. The patriarch was dying and the family split up its members into separate households, sending one child, Aunt Opal, to New York and my grandmother to Hong Kong at age nine. Po Po didn't return to Seattle till she was almost twenty. For those eleven years she was actually Chinese, though the entire time, she insists, she dreamed of eating bread by the fistfuls. And she is still, according to both Chinese and American standards regarding race, really Chinese, where my mother and I might seem to be impostors. She possesses the homogeneity of physical appearance (the same black hair and eyes, her body perhaps a little stouter than the bodies of the Taiwanese from all the bad American food) and cultural values. She understands the appropriate Chinese rules regarding rudeness and civility so ruthlessly employed by waitresses across Taiwan. Po Po married Chinese. Her body stayed faithful. My mother's and mine do not.

In Seattle, Mark longed for sailing harbors and a good bar, "a real pub," he said once, where he could get Newcastle beer. For two weeks last month we went out every night to a different bar by the water, where we would sit and drink pints of lager in silence until I got drunk or Mark tired of the atmosphere and the poor quality of the beer. Then we would go home, fall asleep, and wake the next morning planning for another evening out.

One day, before my mother and I bought tickets to Taiwan, I learned of a disturbing rumor at my college. Several members of the English department felt that the prevailing tone of the university was elitist; people had begun to band in camps of friends that somewhat depended on race and racial sympathies. When I arrived as a student I was not aware of the friction, nor was I close friends with any of the other mixed students in my department, of whom there were only three, at the time. One evening a biracial Latina woman invited me to a dinner party which I could not attend because I was ill. Then I learned of the theory circulating about my absence that night: I was ashamed of being half Chinese. The day I found out about this I met Mark late in the evening at the Blue Unicorn, where he was already working on his third can of Guinness.

"What a load of trash," he said when I told him.

"I don't know how to act now," I said.

"There's nothing to act about. They go around making such a big stink when it doesn't even matter. Half my family comes from France, for God's sake, and I don't care."

"I don't think the Norman conquest counts, Mark."

"Then what does count? You don't look Chinese and you don't speak Chinese. At least I can read French."

"Which you learned in school."

"Your mother doesn't speak Chinese," he said, pushing his chair back.

"This is different."

"How is this different?" he demanded, but I couldn't say.

Later I could articulate the differences between us by telling him that my mother, because of her round and slightly sallow face, her dark hair and eyes, would always be perceived as Asian first. Regardless of her fluency in English, my mother's appearance allows her to be categorized, her experience isolated from that of white America, to be discriminated against in the worst situations. No one in England could simply point to Mark's mother or grandmother and say "French" on first sight. Not without being told.

But at the bar I couldn't articulate any of this because I was recalling something further back, a conversation at my parents' home after dinner when my mother had questioned my father and me about what we might change about our lives had we the opportunity. That night she had surprised us by making a pitcher of margaritas, which we drank during the course of the meal. My mother rarely drinks and hates it when my father consumes more than two martinis at a go. For years she refused to serve alcohol at the house when I visited. "I don't want to condone a bad habit," she had said. "I don't want to be blamed if you become an alcoholic."

"Tell me," she insisted that evening. And, irritated, slightly drunk, I told her I wouldn't want to be half Chinese.

"Full or nothing," I said.

"Fully what?" she asked.

"Whatever," I had replied.

"The fact is, it isn't different," Mark finished and stood to get another beer. "If you married me not one person in England would think you were half Chinese. You want to be different and so you make it a difference." When the waiter came to take his order, he sat back down again, fumbling for his money.

After the bar we went home in a cab which Mark paid for. He told me that his company had started sending letters to the officers in England; soon Mark's yearlong vacation would end and he'd go back to sea. I could see this delighted him and, even though I was still angry, kissed him for congratulations.

That night in bed he tugged my long hair back with his fingers, holding it in place while he fumbled on the nightstand for my hair clip.

"We have to decide what we'll do," I said.

"About the apartment?"

"About staying together."

He brought his lips close to my temples. "I can't afford to get married now," he said.

"I'm not sure I want to get married."

"Fine," he replied.

"Fine," I said. He leaned into me then and his collarbone smelled of lager. "You really should wear your hair back more," he whispered. "You look like a little China doll like that."

When his smell grew too much to stand I sat up violently in bed, pushing him away.

At the National Gallery my mother turns to me in front of the jade cabbage display and announces, "I hope you won't marry Mark."

I had been talking somewhat along the same lines myself the past few days, but it surprises me to hear her say it.

"What don't you like about him?" I ask, and she looks at me.

"He doesn't read, doesn't think, doesn't treat you well," she says. "Doesn't like to do anything but sail and you get sick on boats . . ."

I recalled what Po Po had said the first time I mentioned him.

"It's serious, Po Po," I said. "He's coming from England to visit me."

"Is he white?" she asked.

"Yes," I said.

"That's too bad."

". . . doesn't even think he's in love with you . . ."

"I didn't say that," I say suddenly. "I never said that."

We stop beside a display of ivory miniatures, a tiny woman with white sleeves on a mountain. In the distance lurked a tiger.

"Did Po Po ever tell you not to marry Dad?" I ask.

"Of course not," she says, and I know Po Po didn't have to; my grandmother had refused to speak to my mother when she told her.

"Why do you ask me such embarrassing things?" I demanded.

"What things?"

"You're always asking about our sex life," I say, and my mother's left eye narrows because she can sense we are being watched, overheard, though probably not understood.

"I never ask," she hisses. "You misunderstand my questions."

I walk in frustrated silence for several minutes while she comments glibly about the thousand tiny wood Buddhas stacked in rows, each carving made anonymous by the fact of so many others.

"I just don't understand why you don't like him," I say.

"He exoticizes you," she says finally. "If you want to marry him," she continues, "fine. You can ruin your life with mistakes. After all it doesn't matter what I think about him, it's what you think that makes the difference."

"You just hate him because he's white," I say. She snorts and shakes her head. But her lips close together tightly, as if she is chewing on their delicate inner skin, and I know this is true. In Taipei and at home whenever we see white men with Asian women my mother grimaces complicitously in my direction. I know what she is thinking: *This man is taking advantage of her because she is Chinese.*

It occurs to me now to ask her if she despises my father—the man who had known her for ten years and shyly courted her through college—for loving her, if indeed he does take advantage of her in private because she is Chinese. But I know he doesn't mistreat her; my mother is not docile or shy or subservient. She does not wait to speak until spoken to and she never kowtows. My father is the silent partner in their marriage, the one always trailing a few steps behind.

"Are you sorry you didn't marry Chinese?" I ask.

"What has that got to do with anything?"

"Are you sorry that I'm half?"

"What are you taking about?" she asks angrily, but I can tell that she understands. How much more Chinese we both would have been, I think bitterly, had she married within the community.

I feel like the salesgirl in Sogo with the spidery eyebrows, cheap sweater dangling between my fingers. I can see her fully now; I suddenly understand what she's saying. I have finally been let into the secret.

We've been arguing the whole day: where north is, the best café for tea. This is the third overcast day, and my mother, who packed for warmer weather, is wrapped in a thick sweatshirt she had to buy in order to keep warm. Bundled up this way, it's hard to recognize her in stores or museums. Her appearance makes her anonymous. "I'm freezing," she repeats in the hotel lobby, and I shrug exasperatedly.

It is our next-to-last afternoon in Taipei, and I realize I haven't sent anyone a postcard. Dutifully, I trundle out to the local shop to buy a fistful of cards and can't think of what to write. There is very little that is immediately beautiful about Taipei—only by poring over a map and finding spots like university parks and relatively unvisited temples have we discovered any color, any ornamental relief in this city dominated by high-rises and desolate-looking pockets of houses. Beside the hotel stands a tenement with every window lined with laundry. I keep track of the window toward the far east side, fifth story. Every morning the laundry is different. Today it's four shirts, each white, and a pair of pink shorts. I imagine the woman coming home every night from work and selecting a small portion of the huge laundry pile she must do for the evening. She believes in working in increments; she imagines that by doing just a little every day she can overcome this massive load, never admitting to herself that in a single day she dirties as much as she cleans in a night and so is always stuck in the same place come morning.

When I reach Mark's postcard I can't think of what to write that doesn't sound false or irrelevant. In the end I print, "I'll miss you"; send it, unsigned, from the hotel postbox.

On our last day in Taipei, we both develop hacking coughs that we suspect have more to do with the excessive pollution than the slight flu I caught. To celebrate the end of our vacation I teasingly suggest to Mom that we buy ourselves cotton masks. She glares at me. "Part of growing up," she says, "is learning when to drop it." But we still have to get gifts for family and so we make our way to the market. On the way we find a shop specializing in Thai silks and tablecloths. We go in.

The woman running the shop looks like she'd once spent a significant amount of time in her life following the Grateful Dead. Black bangs completely cover her eyes and she walks around the shop barefoot. Three thick silver bangles slide up and down her tiny arms, covering, the woman insists, "her hideous wrists." My mother and I, sick of each other's company, part immediately at the entrance of the shop, and I go and plant myself in a corner where the saleswoman has stacked ready-made dresses.

My mother fingers everything. The saleswoman speaks rapid-fire Chinese which my mother grunts at, then, guessing that my mother doesn't really understand her, begins typing the prices up on a calculator she has at hand and listing off bits of information in English. I am glad she's caught on to my mother; when their backs are turned I smirk appreciatively at my mother's flustered gestures.

Suddenly my mother turns to me, a full amber-colored cloth draped over her hands. "What do you think?" she asks.

I go over and touch it. "It's beautiful," I say. "How much?"

The saleswoman taps the price into the calculator.

"Buy it," I say.

My mother nods and the woman shuffles off, her patchwork skirt swinging across her feet.

"Visit family here?" she asks as she packs the cloth in paper and I shake my head. We have no family in Taiwan. We know no one in this whole city. She glances over to where my mother sits, hugging herself for warmth. "Your mother?" she asks blandly as I step forward to receive the wrapped package for my mother.

"Yes," I say slowly. The saleswoman nods.

"Different faces, same feelings," she says. My mother coughs and I smile too broadly.

We decide to pretend she is right.

# PART FIVE

# drama

# Shinnob Jep

JIM NORTHRUP

## cast

AL TREEBARK, the host of the game show from the Fond du Lac Reservation. He wears a sport coat made from that camouflage material called Treebark. His necktie is made from red headband material.

FRANKLIN LAKE, a contestant on the show who wears his hair in long braids, has a cowboy hat with mirror sunglasses, an AIM T-shirt, black leather vest, skinny-leg Levis, and cowboy boots. He has a huge beaded watchband and a drumstick hanging out of his pocket.

TRADISH IKWE, a contestant on the show who lives with the seasons on the Fond du Lac Reservation. She wears her hair in a single braid with a quill hair tie. She is wearing a ribbon shirt, ribbon skirt, dream-catcher earrings, and white tennis shoes, no laces.

JOHN JOHNSON, JR., a contestant on the show who was adopted out. He has TV-anchor-styled hair, a blue blazer, gray turtleneck, and slacks. Shiny tassel loafers.

## setting

The stage contains a folding bingo table. It is covered with a white tablecloth that has Ojibwe floral beaded design stencils around the edge. On the table are three podiums with major hotel logos, i.e., Holiday Inn, Radisson, and Motel 6. Each podium has a microphone. The host has a stand-alone podium with a hotel logo. It has a microphone and is decorated with the same stenciled beadwork designs. There are three green powwow toilets used as a green room by the contestants. There is a stand-alone chalkboard that is used to list the categories and dollar amounts. Behind everything is a large stretched hide tied to a log frame. SHINNOB JEP is painted in the center with stenciled beadwork designs around the edge.

As the audience enters they see a dimly lit set and hear singers and a drum. It is a powwow song, a 49 song. As the lights come up, the singers and drum fade. An offstage announcer appears.

The announcer walks in from the back of the audience seats, greeting the crowd. When he gets to the stage he turns and says, "Biindigen! Come in. Welcome to *Shinnob Jep,* the show that tests your knowledge on being a Shinnob. We didn't make our casino connection yet so we're still a low-budget show. Here is your host, Alllllllll Treeeeeeebark."

The announcer now becomes Al as he walks around the podium, taking off a blue headband and putting on a red one that is hanging on the podium.

AL: (*Now facing the audience*) Boozhoo, boozhoo. Good to see you here today. Are there any of my relatives here? (*Hand shading eyes so he can see the audience, sees a relative and waves*) Ever wonder how these contestants for *Shinnob Jep* are picked? Nepotism, pure nepotism. What good is nepotism if you can't nepit? I picked these people to take part. I am always looking for contestants for the show. Remember that blackjack dealer that was here last time? How about if we get a tribal politician next time? Yup, always looking for contestants. Well, let's play *Shinnob Jep.* Our first contestant comes to us from the mean streets of Minneapolis. He is enrolled at White Earth and spends his time at the Peacemaker Center making war on racism. Help me welcome Franklin Lake to *Shinnob Jep!* (*Tucks microphone under arm and leads applause*)

FRANKLIN: (*Comes out of the powwow toilet zipping up, pulls out his drumstick to wave to the crowd*) Boozhoo, brother, I knew I could make it up here. I was just telling Vernand Clyde about this show. (*Gives the audience a clenched-fist salute. The drums make a welcoming sound like at a powwow, drum applause.*)

AL: Our next contestant is from the Fond du Lac Reservation, where she makes syrup in the spring, dances at powwows all summer, goes ricing every fall, and does beadwork all winter. Welcome, Tradish Ikwe, to *Shinnob Jep!* (*The drum makes a welcoming sound, drum applause*)

TRADISH: (*Comes out of her powwow toilet and walks directly to the podium, waves at relatives and friends on both sides of the crowd, then nods at Al*) Boozhoo, Al, good to see you again. How is your ma and dad?

AL: They're good. Our parents went to boarding school together. Last time I saw you was at that powwow in Bena, wasn't it?

TRADISH: (*Cupping a giggle*) Yah, you were there with that blond woman with the big, I mean really big, cameras.

AL: (*Mumbling to the podium*) I remember, I was helping her with a research project.

TRADISH: Oh, is that what they call it nowadays.

AL: (*Trying to silence Tradish using just his eyes, fails*) Daga Bizaan. Let's move on. Our next contestant comes to us from Edina, Minnesota. John is an engineer at Control Data. He just learned that he was adopted by a white couple. He is in the process of enrolling at Leech Lake and finding his real family. Welcome, John Johnson, Jr., to *Shinnob Jep!* (*The drum is tapped softly three times. Tradish and Franklin switch name-plates—because he looks like a Chimook—so he isn't standing between them. John sees it, Al doesn't.*)

JOHN: Hello, Al, I mean Boozhoo. I hope I do well on your show.

AL: I hope so too. We all know how the game is played. Unlike TV's *JEOP-ARDY!*, which does it backwards, here we ask the questions, you give the answers. There is one Daily Double in this round. Here are the categories in the first round of *Shinnob Jep* (*Al points to each category on the chalkboard*): Ricing, Powwows, Tribal Councils, Higher Education, Casinos and Gambling, and Race Relations. John, you lost the toss, you have to go first. Pick a category.

JOHN: I'd like Higher Education for one dollar, Al.

AL: Here's the question—What is the first fiction writing course taken by students?

JOHN: The financial aid forms.

AL: That's right for a dollar. Your choice for categories.

JOHN: Higher Education for two dollars, Al.

AL: OK, why go to summer school?

FRANKLIN: Financial aid all year round.

AL: Correct for two bucks. Pick a category, Franklin.

FRANKLIN: I'd like Race Relations for five dollars, Al.

AL: For five dollars in Race Relations, who invented deodorant because they needed to?

JOHN: The BIA?

AL: Wrong, you're in the hole for four dollars. Who invented deodorant?

FRANKLIN: The white man.

AL: Tha's right for five. Pick again.

FRANKLIN: Tribal councils for three.

AL: The question for three dollars in Tribal Councils is, when do the dead come to life?

TRADISH: Just before the election.

AL: Right, the dead come to life long enough to vote. That's three dollars for Tradish. Your turn to choose.

TRADISH: I'd like Ricing for four hundred, OOPS, I mean four dollars, Al.

AL: Here's the question. What does milky rice mean?

TRADISH: It means you're ricing too early. Jeez, I thought everybody knows that.

AL: Right again, every year some clown sets the opening of the ricing season too early. Pick a category.

TRADISH: Race Relations for three dollars.

AL: For three dollars in Race Relations, respond to the following statement: My grandmother was a Cherokee princess.

TRADISH: Yah, right.

AL: That's wrong. Anyone else?

JOHN: Oh, that's nice.

AL: Correct for three dollars, you're in the hole for two dollars. Pick again.

JOHN: I'd like Race Relations for four, please.

AL: In Race Relations for four, respond to the following statement: My grandmother was a REAL Cherokee princess.

JOHN: Oh, that's nice.

AL: Incorrect, you're five dollars in the hole again. Anyone else want to respond to "My grandmother was a REAL Cherokee princess"?

FRANKLIN: Who gives a fuck?

AL: Who gives a fuck is the right response to "My grandmother was a REAL Cherokee princess." Your turn.

FRANKLIN: Bekaa, am I supposed to use that F-word on your program?

AL: Sure, we'll just pretend this is satellite TV, or cable. Still your turn.

FRANKLIN: Powwows for five, Al.

AL: OK, for five, what is the difference between a contest and a traditional powwow?

FRANKLIN: About a thousand bucks for first place.

AL: Wrong, although we'll check. Nope, the judges say it might be true at some contest powwows but not at all of them. Anyone else want to try? What's the difference between a contest and traditional powwow?

TRADISH: One is for the money and one is for the people.

AL: Right for five bucks. Pick again.

TRADISH: I'll try Ricing for five, Al.

AL: In the category of Ricing, what can you use if you don't have a cast iron parching kettle?

TRADISH: Your neighbor's kettle or a galvanized tub.

AL: Correct. Your turn to pick again, Tradish.

TRADISH: Give me Casinos and Gambling for two dollars.

AL: I was betting we'd never get to this category. OK, for two dollars, what is a good gambling tip?

JOHN: Gas up the car before you get to the casino.

AL: Right, give that man a roll of nickels. Pick again, John.

JOHN: Casinos and Gambling for three dollars.

AL: For three dollars, what is the player's responsibility at the casino?

FRANKLIN: To get as much money as possible.

AL: Hai'. Wrong, although it is a nice wish. Anyone else?

TRADISH: To move the coins from one slot machine to another.

AL: That's right for three dollars.

TRADISH: Let's have Race Relations for two.

AL: The question is, why don't the Chimooks understand the Shinnobs?

TRADISH: They haven't been here long enough.

AL: Sad but true. What has it been? Only five hundred years? Your turn, Tradish.

TRADISH: Casinos and Gambling for four dollars, please.

AL: OK, for two rolls of nickels, what are the odds you'll meet someone you owe money to at the casino?

FRANKLIN: Even money. I know, it happens to me all the time.

AL: Correct for four dollars. Your turn again right after these commercial messages. We got to pay the bills so we can keep playing *Shinnob Jep*. Want to help me, Tradish? C'mon, it's easy. You hold the cards and I'll read the copy.

(*Tradish joins Al at his podium, holds up the first sign that says WAR PONY TOURS.*)

AL: (*Reading*) Hey gamblers, need to get to the casino? Maybe your car was repossessed in a dispute over the payment plan, or your lawyer says to wait before you try driving again. Whatever the problem, War Pony

Tours is the solution. We can make the circuit of Minnesota casinos quicker and better than anyone. One-hour stops at the following casinos: Black Bear, Firefly Creek, Fond du Luth, Fortune Bay, Grand and Grand again, Grand Portage, Jackpot Junction, Lake of the Woods, Little Six, Mystic Lake, Red Lake, River Road, Shooting Star, Treasure Island, and White Oak. We have other rez cars strategically placed so you can continue the trip when the first car dies. Wake up any driver from War Pony Tours for the death ride of your life. War Pony Tours . . . Ho wah.

(*Tradish switches posters to show one that says HOLDEM, ROBBEM, & LEAVEM.*)

AL: (*Reading*) Have your kids been taken away by the county again? Did you set the state record for DWIs, again? You have problems, we have solutions. We've been helping Shinnobs since we found out they could pay their legal bills. The first appointment is free. Call Holdem, Robbem, and Leavem for an appointment. Call 1-800-Shyster. We are an equal opportunity exploiter of the legal system. We've been finding loopholes since 1999.

(*Tradish walks back to her podium and the game resumes.*)

FRANKLIN: I'll try Tribal Councils for four dollars.

AL: For four dollars, why don't incumbents get 100 percent of the vote?

FRANKLIN: It costs too much to buy that many votes.

AL: Correct, it just costs too much. Pick again.

FRANKLIN: I'd like Higher Education for three dollars.

AL: OK, in that category, how long does it take to get a four-year degree?

JOHN: Four years?

AL: Wrong. Anyone else know how long it takes to get a four year degree?

TRADISH: Six to twelve years.

AL: Absolutely right. Another category?

TRADISH: I'll try Ricing for three dollars.

AL: Ricing for three is a Daily Double. You can risk up to twenty bucks. This is an audio Daily Double.

TRADISH: Shoot the works, I'll try twenty.

AL: For twenty bucks, identify the following song. (*A drum, then the sound of the AIM song is heard. Franklin whips out his drumstick and begins to sing along. Tradish is nodding her head in time to the drum. John just looks confused.*) Do you have an answer, Tradish?

TRADISH: Eya', that's the AIM song.

AL: Right again. Pick a category.

TRADISH: Give me Higher Education for four dollars, Al.

AL: OK, for four dollars, what is better than a computer for studying?

JOHN: A really smart roommate.

AL: Right, I used to have one. Your turn.

JOHN: Tribal Councils for five dollars, Al.

AL: For five, how many relatives of the tribal council does it take to cut the grass?

TRADISH: Two or three.

AL: Gaawiin, anyone else want to try? How many relatives of the tribal council does it take to cut the grass?

JOHN: All of them.

AL: Eya', it takes all of the relatives to cut the grass. Next category, please.

JOHN: I'd like Tribal Councils for two bucks.

AL: What is plan B to ensure the outcome of the election?

JOHN: Election boards appointed by the tribal councils.

AL: That's right for two bucks. Give that man another roll of nickels. Another category?

JOHN: I want Casinos and Gambling for five, Al.

AL: How do you start a fight in a casino?

JOHN: Sit next to a nonsmoker.

AL: Correct, just sit next to a nonsmoker. Your turn.

JOHN: Higher Education for five, Al.

AL: What's better, a grant or loan for college?

JOHN: A grant, at least that's what worked for me.

AL: Right you are. Pick again, please.

JOHN: Race Relations for a dollar, Al.

AL: The last question in Race Relations is, do you mind if I ask what ah, tribe, ah band, ah group you belong to?

TRADISH: No.

AL: Incorrect. A good answer but not the one we're looking for. Anyone else? Do you mind if I ask what ah, tribe, ah band, ah group you belong to?

JOHN: Yes, I do mind.

AL: Correct for one dollar. Pick again.

JOHN: I'd like Powwows for four dollars, please.

AL: In that category, name four things that contribute to a good powwow.

JOHN: Good dancers, good drums, a lot of giveaways, and honor songs.

AL: Good answer but not the one we're looking for. Anyone else?

FRANKLIN: Good water, good food stands, a quiet place to camp, and freshly pumped powwow toilets.

AL: Close enough. Your turn, Franklin.

FRANKLIN: Ho wah! I'll try Powwows for three, Al.

AL: OK, for three bucks, who comes after the traditional men dancers in most grand entries?

FRANKLIN: The grass dancers.

AL: Keereckt for three. Pick again.

FRANKLIN: Give me Tribal Councils for one dollar, Al.

AL: You can't buy a tribal council for one dollar, it takes much more than that. Seriously, for one dollar in that category, who gave us tribal councils?

JOHN: The federal government.

AL: Right, the 1934 Indian Reorganization Act. Your turn to choose.

JOHN: Casinos and Gambling for one dollar.

AL: For one dollar, should you hate someone who wins on a slot machine you just left?

JOHN: No, it's never right to hate someone.

AL: Gaawiin, haven't played the slot machines much, have you? That'll cost you a dollar. Does anyone else want to try? Should you hate someone who wins on a slot machine you just left?

FRANKLIN: Eya', for a little while anyway.

AL: Correctemondo, give that man a half roll of nickels. OK, before we get started on Shinnob Double Jep, let's chat with the contestants and recap the scores. Tradish is leading with thirty-six dollars, John is second with twenty dollars, and Franklin is sucking hind tit with sixteen bucks. Franklin, on your card it says you're enrolled at White Earth. Tell us an election story.

FRANKLIN: Well, one time my cousin and I were guarding the cemetery, but the dead got by us and voted the same dictator into office again. I liked voting last election. I voted sixteen times. My cousin was greedier and voted twenty-three times. At one hundred bucks a vote, we both made money on that election. I like getting Ben Franklins for Franklin during elections.

AL: Thank you for sharing that with us, but shouldn't you be telling that story to the inspector general of the Interior Department?

FRANKLIN: I already did. They interviewed me several times and I may get called to testify in federal court.

AL: Thanks, we'll be looking for you in the newspapers. John, your card says you just found out that you were once a Shinnob but were raised white. Did that make it hard for you?

JOHN: Sometimes. Now I understand why I wanted to choke my sister's rabbit. It wasn't violence, it was hereditary. I never get sunburnt like the rest of the family either. In the family photo album, I stick out like a blueberry in a glass of milk. I'm looking to find what was taken from me. I'm taking day courses in Indian studies and night courses in the language. I'll visit my adopted parents but will connect with my real family.

AL: That's great, John, glad to have you back with us. Tradish, on your card under marital status it says unremarried. Does that mean we can try again?

TRADISH: Nah, you had your chance. Where is your blond with the big cameras?

AL: I ended before the project did. We don't see each other anymore. Enough about her, what are you doing this weekend?

TRADISH: I'll be washing my hare, my snowshoe hare. Seriously, what did you have in mind for the weekend? I might be around.

AL: Well, Rabbit Choker, they have bingo at the Black Bear Casino. Want to join me? They gave me some packages for mentioning their name on the show. You still like bingo, don't you?

TRADISH: Yah, I like bingo at the Black Bear. I can join you there Friday night, Saturday afternoon and evening, Sunday afternoon and evening.

FRANKLIN: Hey, this is *Shinnob Jep*, not the *Dating Game*. Aaniin dina?

AL: Gaawiin gegoo. Now that we got that squared away, let's go back to the game. The categories in this round are U.S. History, Trick or Treaties, Trick or Treatment, Body Language, Sugar Bush, and Rez Cars. Franklin, you gave me the last correct answer so it's your turn again. Pick one.

FRANKLIN: I'll try U.S. History for one dollar, Al.

AL: For one dollar, who defeated General George Armstrong Custer at the Battle of the Little Big Horn?

FRANKLIN: That's an easy one, Crazy Horse, a Lakota.

AL: That's right. Pick again.

FRANKLIN: Give me Rez Cars for a dollar.

AL: Here we go. Who never drove a rez car?

FRANKLIN: Crazy Horse, a Lakota.

AL: Correct. Your turn again.

FRANKLIN: I'd like Trick or Treatment for a buck.

AL: For one dollar, who never went to treatment?

FRANKLIN: Crazy Horse, a Lakota.

AL: Boy, you really know these subjects, don't you? Go ahead, pick another one.

FRANKLIN: I want Trick or Treaties for a dollar.

AL: Name a famous Indian who fought during treaty signing times.

FRANKLIN: This is too easy, Crazy Horse, a Lakota.

AL: Once again, that is the answer we were looking for. It's still your turn, Franklin.

FRANKLIN: Give me Rez Cars for two dollars.

AL: For two bucks, what is the payment plan for a rez car?

FRANKLIN: Everything down and nothing a month for the life of the car.

AL: Are you gonna let anyone else play? But speaking of a payment plan, we have to take another commercial break here. (*Tradish comes over without being asked to help with the commercials. John goes to his green room. She holds up the Niiwin placard while Al reads from a card.*)

AL: Got a big giveaway coming up? Talk to Niiwin from Niiwin's Tipi Poles. He makes balsam and tamarack poles for tipis. They are hand made, up to forty foot in length, and are smooth as a politician's promise. Niiwin likes bartering so he'll trade poles for damn near anything: money, wild rice, money, traditional dance regalia, money, bingo packages, money. He has rentals and loaners. Tipi poles do make an ideal gift for those relatives who get gambling per capita and have everything. When you need something to hold all that canvas up, try Niiwin's Tipi Poles. Remember, our poles are biodegradable and will not harm the environment. (*A toilet-flushing noise is heard and John comes out and returns to his podium. Al holds up the Boogid placard as Tradish reads the next commercial.*)

TRADISH: Have the kids been playing swordfighter with your knockers again? Has your old pole seen one too many seasons? Boogid's Wild Rice Tools is the answer. We're always ready for ricing because we make professional-grade tools at mud-bottom prices. At Boogid's, we use straight-grain white cedar for the knockers and measure them to fit. Our spruce/diamond willow poles can almost be used to push a Lake Superior ore boat. At Boogid's, we make ricing tools your grandchildren will fight over. As my grampa used to say, ricing is never more than eleven months away.

AL: Go ahead, Franklin. It's still your turn.

FRANKLIN: I'm on a roll here. Rez Cars for three, please.

AL: Will a Chevy wheel fit on a Ford car?

FRANKLIN: No, it will not.

AL: Hai'. Wrong answer. Anyone else want to try? Will a Chevy wheel fit on a Ford car?

TRADISH: I suppose, if your hammer is big enough.

AL: Eya'. Tradish, pick your category.

TRADISH: Rez Cars for four dollars, Al.

AL: In that category, what do you use to replace a broken radio antenna?

TRADISH: A wire coat hanger.

AL: Good answer. Your turn again.

TRADISH: U.S. History for two, please.

AL: For two dollars, who invented the BIA?

FRANKLIN: Someone who was really mad at us.

AL: Right. Your turn to choose.

FRANKLIN: We haven't done Body Language yet. I'll try that one for two bucks.

AL: Demonstrate someone giving directions. How would you say, that way and around the corner to the right?

TRADISH: Like this. (*Lips and chin pointing straight ahead, then lips turning to the right*)

AL: That's right. You could get a job as a tour guide. Or at a kissing booth. Your turn.

TRADISH: I'll try Trick or Treatment for two dollars, Al.

AL: Here's the question, why go to treatment?

FRANKLIN: Job security for my cousin Wiinug, the counselor.

AL: We'll accept that. Choose again.

FRANKLIN: Trick or Treaties for three, Al.

AL: OK, how can we improve the treaty-making process?

JOHN: We write them in our language, then tell the president what it says after he signs it.

FRANKLIN: Ho wah, good answer, niij.

AL: That's right, I wish we could have done that with all of them. Pick again, John.

JOHN: Trick or Treatment for three.

AL: In that category, what is the thirteenth AA step?

JOHN: To quit bragging about the previous twelve steps.

AL: Correct. Your turn to choose.

JOHN: I'd like U.S. History for three dollars.

AL: OK, for three bucks in U.S. History, who did you cheer for during the Civil War?

FRANKLIN: Both sides.

AL: Right again. Your category, please.

FRANKLIN: U.S. History for four bucks.

AL: For four bucks, who invented canoes?

FRANKLIN: We did. Ho wah, nitaawichige.

AL: That's a good answer. Pick another one.

FRANKLIN: Trick and Treaties for two frogskins.

AL: How long does the grass grow and the river flow?

FRANKLIN: Until the white man needs the land and water.

AL: Eya', that's right. Your turn to choose.

FRANKLIN: That was a good one. Trick or Treaties for four, please.

AL: That's one of the two Daily Doubles. You have thirty-two dollars. You can risk the entire amount, if you like.

FRANKLIN: Do it all. We didn't come in here half-stepping.

AL: OK, the category this time is Commods Spanish. Provide the English translation: degermed *harina de maíz*.

FRANKLIN: The answer is enriched yellow corn meal.

AL: Eya', that's correct. You now have sixty-four dollars. Pick again.

FRANKLIN: We haven't tried Sugar Bush. Give me that one for a dollar, please.

AL: For one dollar, how did you know he was new at the Sugar Bush?

JOHN: He was tapping a basswood tree.

AL: Eya', your pick.

JOHN: Sugar Bush for two.

AL: In that category, how did you know he was new at the Sugar Bush?

JOHN: He kept looking for a bush made of sugar.

AL: Eya', pick again.

JOHN: Sugar Bush for three, please.

AL: For three bucks, how did you know he was new at the Sugar Bush?

JOHN: He kept saying, "Why do you do this? You can buy syrup at the store."

AL: Eya', we like that answer. Try again.

JOHN: I like this category. Four dollars in Sugar Bush.

AL: OK, how did you know he was new at the Sugar Bush?

JOHN: He burnt himself while playing with the fire.

AL: Eya'. How do you know these things? I thought you were from Edina and worked at Control Data.

JOHN: I am from Edina, but I went to the Sugar Bush for the first time this year and I made all those mistakes. Can I have the last question in that category?

AL: OK, for five bucks. The question this time is, how did you know he was new at the Sugar Bush?

JOHN: He went home before noon.

AL: Eya', that's right. You cleaned up in this category. Pick another one.

JOHN: I'll try Body Language for three, please.

AL: For three bucks, how did you know she was mad at him?

FRANKLIN: She was staring daggers and making fists at him with her hands in her pockets.

AL: That's right. Franklin, I thought you went to sleep over there, glad to see you back in the game. OK, your turn to choose a category.

FRANKLIN: Trick or Treatment for four, Al.

AL: The question is, quote the source: He was taking my inventory.

TRADISH: That's from the AA's fourth step, Al.

AL: Eya'. Absolutely right, way to go. Your turn, Tradish.

TRADISH: I'd like Trick or Treaties for five, Al.

AL: That is the other Daily Double. You have forty-two dollars. You can risk the entire amount.

TRADISH: Nah, since I was eighteen when we first went out, I'll bet eighteen dollars.

AL: Now that is a good reason. The category is Commods Spanish. Provide the English translation for *jarabe de maíz*.

TRADISH: Easy beans, that's corn syrup.

AL: Right again, you're really smart. You're now tied with Franklin at sixty-seven dollars. Pick again, we have a few questions left.

FRANKLIN: Still trying to snag, Al?

AL: Bangii etago, maybe a little bit. Pick me, I mean, pick a category, Tradish.

TRADISH: U.S. History for five, you old rat hide.

AL: I didn't think you cared enough to call me a rat hide, thanks. Oh yah, we're in the middle of a game here. For five bucks in U.S. History, say one swear word.

JOHN: Manifest Destiny.

AL: Correct. Your turn, John.

JOHN: I'd like Rez Cars for five, Al.

AL: Here we go. Tell me a rez car story.

JOHN: I'm at a little bit of a handicap here because I drive a Volvo station wagon, the 340 DL model, but I heard one last week. Let's see if I got this right. . . . "I knocked a hole in one of the pistons, and every time I cranked it, the dipstick would come shooting out of the engine. It was fun until the dipstick hit a highway patrolman's car."

AL: Wow, not bad. Told just like the owner of a rez car. We'll give you five bucks for that story. Pick again.

JOHN: Body Language for five.

AL: Demonstrate one way Shinnobs greet each other in a crowd.

JOHN: I saw two Shinnobs doing this yesterday at the Mall of America. (*Eye contact, then tilting the head back and forth one-half inch*).

AL: Close enough, I'd nod back at you. That answer is good for five bucks. It's still your turn.

JOHN: Trick or Treaties for four, Al.

AL: All right, who owns the rights guaranteed in the treaties?

JOHN: Not the tribal governments but the generations of Anishinaabe to come, the ones not born yet.

AL: Great answer. I want to give you four dollars of my own money for that answer.

TRADISH: I'll chip in three myself.

FRANKLIN: Me too, niijii, here's my three bucks.

AL: All right, that leaves both of you with sixty-four dollars. John, you now have sixty-one bucks. We're running out of time here, pick a question.

JOHN: I'd like Body Language for three, please.

AL: Demonstrate the stroke used to knock rice.

JOHN: I saw this in one of the movies at the university. (*Reaches out for the rice with his left hand, then strokes the rice with his right hand, which then reaches out for the rice, which is stroked twice. He repeats until stopped by Al.*)

AL: Bekaa, bekaa. Are you sure you haven't been ricing before? It looked like you were on your way to three sacks, at least. That brings your total to sixty-four dollars. That's the end of this round. We have the Shinnob Final Jep question in this category, Commods Spanish. Write down your wagers and answers for this question. Ready? Translate this into English: Leche instantanea en polvo sin grasa. (*Tradish and Franklin write down their wagers and answers to the question. They both show their answers to John, who then writes his answer.*) Time's up. John, show us your answer.

JOHN: I wrote down Instant Nonfat Dry Milk and wagered it all.

AL: That gives you 128 dollars. Franklin, show us your answer and the amount you wagered.

FRANKLIN: I did the same thing as he did. I bet it all. Here is my answer. (*Holds up a paper showing the words* Instant Nonfat Dry Milk) Ho waa!

AL: You're tied with John at 128 dollars. Tradish, don't tell me you did the same thing too?

TRADISH: Sure, that was an easy one because I use it all the time in my fry bread. I bet sixty-four dollars too. (*Shows her wager and answer that says* Instant Nonfat Dry Milk)

AL: It looks like we have a tie game here. Nobody loses, you're all winners. Thank you for playing our game. Thank you all for coming to *Shinnob Jep.* Mii gwech, Tradish, can I have your phone number?

TRADISH: Sure, bekaa. (*She takes a piece of birchbark out of her pocket, folds it, bites it, looks at it, refolds it, and bites it again. When she is done, she hands her phone number to Al.)*

FRANKLIN: Hey John, we're starting a new drum group at the Peacemaker Center. Want to join us and learn how to sing? Maybe we can hit a few powwows this summer.

JOHN: That'd be great. Here is my card with all my numbers—home, office, cell, beeper, fax, and my e-mail address. Will we see you there, Tradish?

TRADISH: Maybe. Why don't you stop by the house next fall? We can show you how to make rice, you know, finish it the old-time way. (*Gives Al the nod, the nod that means let's get away from all these people so we can talk alone*)

AL: I've never seen a three-way tie before. I wonder why it happened?

JOHN: Maybe when you share information and wisdom, we all win.

Mii sa iw.

# contributors

**Sherman Alexie,** a Spokane/Coeur d'Alene Indian, grew up on the Spokane Indian Reservation in Wellpinit, Washington, about fifty miles northwest of Spokane. He is the author of the novels *Reservation Blues* and *Indian Killer*, and he wrote the award-winning screenplay for *Smoke Signals*, a film based on his short-story collection *The Lone Ranger and Tonto Fistfight in Heaven*. His recent books include the short-story collection *The Toughest Indian in the World* and the poetry collection *One Stick Song*. In 1998, Alexie participated with seven others in the PBS *Lehrer NewsHour Dialogue on Race* with President Clinton. One of *Granta's* "Twenty Best American Novelists under the Age of 40," Alexie has had his work appear in numerous publications and anthologies, including *Best American Short Stories*. He resides with his wife and son in Seattle, Washington.

**Peter Bacho's** first novel, *Cebu*, won a 1992 American Book Award. His collection of short stories *Dark Blue Suit* won a Washington State Governor's Writers Award and the Murray Morgan Prize. His other publications include a nonfiction work, *Boxing in Black and White* (1999), and a second novel, *Nelson's Run* (2001).

**Nick Carbó** is the author of two volumes of poetry, *El Grupo McDonald's* (1995) and *Secret Asian Man* (2000). He is the editor of *Returning a Borrowed Tongue: An Anthology of Filipino and Filipino American Poetry* (1996). Among his awards are fellowships in poetry from the National Endowment for the Arts and the New York Foundation for the Arts. He lives in Miami with his wife, who is also a poet.

**Daniel Chacón** has been published in such journals as *Calalloo*, the *New England Review*, *Colorado Review*, *Clackamas Literary Review*, and *ZYZZYVA*. His first book, *Chicano Chicanery*, in which "Godoy Lives" appears, was put out by Arte Público Press (2000). From Fresno, California, he currently teaches in the M.F.A. Creative Writing Program at the University of Texas, El Paso.

**Lucille Clifton** was born in Depew, New York, in 1936. Her books of poetry include *Blessing the Boats: New and Selected Poems 1988–2000* (2000), which won the National Book Award; *The Terrible Stories* (1995), which was nominated for the National Book Award; *The Book of Light* (1993); *Quilting: Poems 1987–1990* (1991); *Next: New Poems* (1987); *Good Woman: Poems and a Memoir 1969–1980* (1987), which was nominated for the Pulitzer Prize; *Two-Headed Woman* (1980), also a Pulitzer Prize nominee and winner of the University of Massachusetts Press Juniper Prize; *An Ordinary Woman* (1974); *Good News about the Earth* (1972); and *Good Times* (1969). She has also written *Generations: A Memoir* (1976) and more than sixteen books for children. Her honors include an Emmy Award from the American Academy of Television Arts and Sciences, a Lannan Literary Award, two fellowships from the National Endowment for the Arts, the Shelley Memorial Award, and the YM-YWHA Poetry Center Discovery Award. In 1999 she was elected a chancellor of the Academy of American Poets. She has served as poet laureate for the state of Maryland and is currently distinguished professor of humanities at St. Mary's College of Maryland.

**Ray Gonzalez** is a poet, essayist, and editor born in El Paso, Texas. He is the author of *Memory Fever* (1999), a memoir about growing up in the Southwest; *Turtle Pictures* (2000), a prose poem memoir; *The Ghost of John Wayne and Other Stories* (2001); and *The Underground Heart: Essays from Hidden Landscapes* (2002). He is also the author of seven books of poetry, including *The Heat of Arrivals* (1997 PEN/Oakland Josephine Miles Book Award), *Cabato Sentora* (1999 Minnesota Book Award Finalist), and the forthcoming *The Hawk Temple at Tierra Grande*. His work has appeared in *Best American Poetry*, *The Pushcart Prize: Best of the Small Presses 2000*, *The Norton Anthology of Nature Writing*, and *Best American Nature Writing*. Gonzalez is the editor of twelve anthologies, most recently *Touching the Fire: Fifteen Poets of the Latino Renaissance* (1998). He has served as poetry editor of the *Bloomsbury Review* for twenty years and recently founded a poetry journal, *LUNA*. He is associate professor with an endowed chair, the McKnight Land Grant Professorship, at the University of Minnesota in Minneapolis.

**Gish Jen** grew up in Scarsdale, New York, the daughter of Chinese immigrant parents. Her first novel, *Typical American*, published in 1991, became a *New York Times* "Notable Book of the Year." Her second novel, *Mona in the Promised Land* (1996), was also a *New York Times* "Notable Book of the Year" and was named one of the top ten best books of 1996 by the *Los Angeles Times*. Both books were finalists for the National Book Critics Circle Award. Her shorter works have appeared in the *Atlantic Monthly*, the *New Yorker*, the *New*

*Republic* and the *New York Times*. Many of her award-winning stories, including "Birthmates," were collected in *Who's Irish?* in 1999. Jen has been awarded fellowships from the Guggenheim Foundation, Radcliffe College's Bunting Institute, the National Endowment for the Arts, and the MacDowell Colony. She earned a B.A. in English from Harvard University in 1977 and an M.F.A. from the Iowa Writers' Workshop in 1983.

**Charles Johnson,** a 1998 MacArthur Fellow, received the National Book Award for his novel *Middle Passage* in 1990. He has also published three other novels—*Dreamer* (1998), *Oxherding Tale* (1982), and *Faith and the Good Thing* (1974)—and two story collections, *The Sorcerer's Apprentice* (1986) and *Soulcatcher* (2001). Among his many books are *King: The Photobiography of Martin Luther King, Jr.* (coauthored with Bob Adelman, 2000), *Africans in America: America's Journey through Slavery* (coauthored with Patricia Smith, 1998), *Being and Race: Black Writing since 1970* (1988), *Black Men Speaking* (coedited with John McCluskey, Jr., 1997), and two books of drawings, *Black Humor* (1970) and *Half-Past Nation Time* (1972). Among his many awards is the Lifetime Achievement in the Arts Award from the Corporate Council for the Arts. In 1999 Indiana University published a "reader" of his work entitled *I Call Myself an Artist: Writings by and about Charles Johnson*. A literary critic, screenwriter, philosopher, international lecturer, and cartoonist with more than one thousand drawings published, he is the S. Wilson and Grace M. Pollock Endowed Professor of English at the University of Washington in Seattle.

**Allison Joseph** teaches at Southern Illinois University, where she also serves as poetry editor of the *Crab Orchard Review* and director of the Young Writers Workshop, a writing conference for high school students. Her books include *What Keeps Us Here*, *Soul Train*, and *In Every Seam*.

**Sandra Tsing Loh** is a writer-performer whose two off-Broadway solo shows include *Bad Sex with Bud Kemp* and *Aliens in America*, at Second Stage Theatre. Loh has been featured at HBO's U.S. Comedy Arts Festival in Aspen and on two National Public Radio programs, *Morning Edition* and Ira Glass's *This American Life*. Her books include *Depth Takes a Holiday: Essays from Lesser Los Angeles*, *Aliens in America*, and a novel, *If You Lived Here, You'd Be Home by Now*, which was named by the *Los Angeles Times* as one of the best books of 1997. Her solo piano CD *Pianovision* was produced by K2B2 Records.

**Erika Lopez** is author of four graphic novels and collections: *Hoochie Mama: The Other White Meat*; *They Call Me Mad Dog: A Story for Bitter, Lonely*

*People*; *Flaming Iguanas: An All-Girl Road Novel Thing*; and *Lap Dancing for Mommy: Tender Stories of Disgust, Blame, and Inspiration.*

**John McNally** is the author of the short-story collection *Troublemakers*, winner of the John Simmons Short Fiction Award in 2000. He has edited two other anthologies, *The Student Body: Short Stories about College Students and Professors* (2001) and *High Infidelity: 24 Great Short Stories about Adultery* (1997). He is the Jenny McKean Moore fellow at George Washington University in Washington, D.C., where he lives with his wife, Amy Knox Brown, their three dogs, Yogi, Lucille, and Emma, and their two cats, Ashley and Jordan.

**Aimee Nezhukumatathil** is the author of a chapbook, *Fishbone*, winner of the Snail's Pace Press Award. Her poetry collection *Miracle Fruit* won the Tupelo Press first book prize and will appear in 2002. Her poems and essays have appeared in *Chelsea*, the *Southern Review*, *Beloit Poetry Journal*, *Quarterly West*, and *Mid-American Review*. A former fellow at the Wisconsin Institute for Creative Writing, she currently teaches creative writing at SUNY College at Fredonia.

**Jim Northrup,** Anishinaabe, writes the syndicated column "Fond du Lac Follies," which is distributed in the *Circle*, the *Native American Press*, and *News from Indian Country*. "Fond du Lac Follies" was named best column at the 1999 Native American Journalists Association convention. His books include *Rez Road Follies: Canoes, Casinos, Computers, and Birch Bark Baskets* and *Walking the Rez Road*. From 1990 to 1992, Jim worked as a roster artist for the COMPAS Writer-in-the-Schools Program. He has been a mentor in the Loft Inroads Program, a judge for the Lake Superior Contemporary Writers Series and the Jerome Fellowship, and a member of the Minnesota State Arts Board Prose Panel. Northrup also has given radio commentaries on the Superior Radio Network, National Public Radio, Fresh Air Radio, and the BBC-Scotland. He and his family live the traditional life of the Anishinaabe in northern Minnesota.

**Paisley Rekdal,** the daughter of a Chinese American mother and a Norwegian father, was born and raised in Seattle, Washington. She is the author of an essay collection, *The Night My Mother Met Bruce Lee*. Her collection of poetry, *A Crash of Rhinos*, was published as part of the University of Georgia Press's Contemporary Poetry Series. Her poems and essays have appeared in numerous magazines, including *Poetry Northwest*, the *Sonora Review*, and

*Grand Tour*. A past recipient of Fulbright and Hopwood awards, she teaches at the University of Wyoming.

**Tim Seibles** is the author of five books of poetry: *Body Moves* (1988), *Hurdy Gurdy* (1992), *Kerosene* (1995), *Ten Miles an Hour* (1998) and *Hammerlock* (1999). He has received fellowships from the Provincetown Fine Arts Work Center and the National Endowment for the Arts, and he won an Open Voice Award from the National Writers' Voice Project. His poems have appeared in numerous places, including *Ploughshares, New England Review, Kenyon Review, Black American Literature Forum*, and the anthologies *In Search of Color Everywhere* and *New American Poets in the '90s*. He currently teaches in the M.F.A. creative writing program at Old Dominion University in Norfolk, Virginia.

**Michele Serros,** born in Oxnard, California, was still a student at Santa Monica College when her first book of poetry and short stories, *Chicana Falsa*, was published. When Lalo Press, the original publisher, went out of business, Serros sold copies of the book from her garage, and since then *Chicana Falsa* has become required reading in high schools and universities nationwide. An award-winning poet and commentator for National Public Radio's *Morning Edition* and *Weekend All Things Considered*, Serros has released a spoken-word CD on Mercury Records and toured with Lollapalooza as a "road poet." She was selected by the Getty Research Institute and the Poetry Society of America to have her poetry placed on MTA buses throughout Los Angeles County. She has also been a featured contributor for the *Los Angeles Times*'s children's fiction section. Serros's collection of fiction, *How to Be a Chicana Role Model* (2000), quickly reached the *Los Angeles Times* bestseller list. She was recently named by *Newsweek* as "one of the top young women to watch for in the new century." Currently living in New York City, Serros is working on a young adult novel tentatively titled *Notes for a Medium Brown Girl*. She continues to speak at high schools, correctional facilities, and universities across the country.

# permissions